W9-CUW-525

Clinical Supervision: Legal, Ethical, and Risk Management Issues

George B. Haarman, Psy.D., LMFT

Copyright © 2013 George Haarman

All Rights Reserved

First Published in the United States in 2013 by:
Foundations: Education & Consultation

FOR INFORMATION ADDRESS:

Foundations: Education & Consultation

1400 Browns Lane

Louisville, Kentucky 40207

Copyright © 2012 by George B. Haarman, Psy.D.

All Rights Reserved. No part of this publication may be reproduced or transmitted in any form or by any means, electronic or mechanical, including photocopying, recording, or any information or storage retrieval system now known or to be invented, without permission in writing from the publisher, except by a reviewer who wishes to quote brief passages.

ISBN: 978-1482636048

For the women in my life: my wife, my daughters, and my granddaughters

Table of Contents

CHAPTER ONE
Competent and Effective Clinical Supervision

Ten Myths Regarding Clinical Supervision

Supervision is a process that is known by many, but understood by few. Many misconceptions and misunderstandings exist regarding the nature of clinical supervision. Traditionally clinical supervision has been an integral part of the training process for many human service professionals. Yet, while supervision was an integral part of professional training and improvement of service delivery, few supervisors and supervisees fully understood the process. Misconceptions have been perpetuated by individuals who have been unprepared for acting as a supervisor and have received little or no formal training in supervision. As a result, when supervisees became supervisors, many of the same misconceptions became perpetuated and further muddled.

Supervision Myths (Campbell, 2006)

1. If I am an experienced counselor or psychotherapist, I automatically will be successful and effective as a supervisor.

2. True clinical supervision is strictly for the review of cases. If you give handouts or teach, that's training, not supervision.

3. If supervision is not going well, it's the supervisee's fault.

4. Supervision is only for the beginners or inexperienced. If you have to be supervised you must be deficient/incompetent.

5. Because supervisors are professionals, diversity issues do not have to be addressed.

6. The best feedback is direct. Tell it like you see it. There is no need to coddle supervisees.

7. A supervisee's thoughts and feeling are not relevant to learning.

8. Supervisors are experts, so it is important to make that clear and never admit to mistakes or that you don't know the answer.

9. Because supervisors are totally responsible for the actions of their supervisees, the supervisor's directions should not be questioned.

10. In order to avoid a dual relationship and becoming your supervisee's therapist, you shouldn't use your therapy skills in supervision.

Probably the biggest myth about supervision is the illusion that, just because I am a veteran therapist or counselor or just because I'm an experienced clinician, I will automatically make a good supervisor. In many situations, individuals who were very good clinicians turned out to be very poor supervisors. The skill set required for each job is significantly different. Knowledge and skills in service provision are required for both, but the skills, abilities, interests, and temperament required to be a supervisor are very different. The skills that are required for a therapist or counselor and the skill set for clinical supervisors share some commonality, but the tasks to be accomplished and the desired outcomes are different. *Just because you are a good counselor does not mean that you have the skills to be a good supervisor.*

Another misconception involves viewing clinical supervision strictly as a review of cases.. Refiewing cases and monitoring for compliance on the part of the worker is a very limited concept of supervision. It ignores one of the key components of what good clinical supervision is about, specifically, professional development. Supervision also includes a number of other core dimensions, including the growth of the individual, the growth of the profession, safeguarding the profession, and ensuring the quality of services for clients. *Good supervision goes well beyond simply reviewing cases records and co-signing forms and reports.*

Some individuals have mistakenly viewed supervision as an activity for beginners or for professionals of questionable skills. "I have been in this field for 20 years and I don't need to be supervised anymore. I am quite capable functioning without supervision." Supervision, in some situations, has been mistakenly viewed as punitive, a misconception that may be inadvertently promulgated by licensing board actions.

Typically, whenever individuals are brought up for disciplinary action by state licensing boards, a frequent part of the resolution of their case may require the individual to be under supervision for a specified period of time. If a professional displays a lapse in judgment or behaves improperly, the licensing board is very likely to require that professional to function under the watchful eye of a supervisor who reports to the board. In those situations, supervision has been the equivalent of a statement of fact that a professional was not competent or effective and required additional oversight. This has made supervision feel punitive, rather than appropriately understanding that the nature of supervision is much broader. *Supervision is*

7

desirable at all experience levels to ensure service quality.

Another misconception regarding supervision has revolved around issues of diversity and culture. Just because I am a trained and veteran professional, doesn't mean that I don't have to be concerned about how diversity issues impact my supervision. A faulty assumption is that, simply because we are both professionals, we ought to be able to deal with diversity issues and cultural differences. As a good supervisor, you have to be concerned about diversity and culture and their impact on the supervisory interaction. It is a fundamentally different dynamic, as a white male, when I'm supervising another white male as compared to when I'm supervising an Asian female. Unacknowledged acculturation factors make the dynamics of each supervision *szaware of and attempts to address diversity issues in supervision.*

Some supervisors have had the misconception that the best way to supervise is to control, dictate, and micromanage to prevent the possibility of a "screw up" or harm to a client. This misconception has resulted in an attitude of "don't coddle supervisees." This approach was to simply wait for them to screw up, and then make them understand how incompetent they are so they won't make the same mistake again. The supervisor presents herself as the "expert" who knows everything. The best supervisors may be those who can acknowledge that "I really am not competent in that area, but I'll find out or perhaps we both need to do some reading on that issue." Unfortunately some supervisors felt like they had to present themselves as the guru and the "be-all and end-all" in any supervisory situation. This posture or attitude may not have served their supervisees well, because the supervisor was faking it instead of really being genuine about the process of supervision. *Supervision is an interactive process between two professionals (or a professional in training) that can only reach its true potential when both parties participate openly and fully.*

One of the most common misconceptions of supervision, that is still fairly prevalent, was viewing supervision as therapy. During the 70's and 80's, supervision was viewed and practiced in very similar terms as psychotherapy. The supervisor's role was to "therapize" the supervisee to the point that one could safely assume that the supervisee would not be imposing their issues on the clients. In many instances, supervision looked and felt a great deal like self-exploration, self-development, or a therapy session. The emphasis was on the supervisee's development and working through their personal issues. Very little emphasis was placed on skill development, professional development, or providing high quality services to the client..

A gradual awareness emerged that the emphasis of supervision should be about learning skills to provide a high quality service to clients, not purging supervisees of their personal demons. The pendulum has now swung to the other side, to the point that everyone is generally clear that supervision should not be therapy. Nevertheless, in order to protect clients, we cannot ignore the emotional issues or psychopathology of the supervisee, but it may be more appropriate to refer the supervisee out to someone else for therapeutic services.

The pendulum has swung so far, that some people believe that as a supervisor, I have to park my clinical skills at the door and simply become an automaton case reviewer.   Active listening, reframing, partializing , and decatastroposizing are good skills in terms of simple human interaction and supervision as well as psychotherapy. *Employing and utilizing those therapeutic skills in a therapy situation is very different than the purpose that you would use those skills for in supervision. Nevertheless it is not inappropriate to utilize those basic skills as a part of the supervision process.*

Clinical Supervision

There are a myriad of different definitions of clinical supervision. One that I view as particularly clear and concise is put forth by Campbell (2006). "Clinical supervision is the process of reviewing and monitoring a practitioner's work to increase their skills and to help them solve problems in order to provide clients the optimal quality of service possible, and to prevent harm from occurring." Campbell's definition identified the key element of clinical supervision as reviewing and monitoring. As a supervisor you are responsible for monitoring the quality of services that are being provided by your supervisee. The supervisor is in charge of quality control and quality control cannot be achieved without regularly monitoring and regularly reviewing the work of those that you supervise.

Another role that supervisors play, in addition trying to be the quality control engineer, is that of the training and development officer. Part of the supervisory function is to make sure that supervisees grow and develop into the best practitioner that they can be given their particular set of talents and skills. Supervision is more than just being a person who sits there with a stack of case files and checks on whether or not a supervisee is providing acceptable services.

A major aspect of the role of a supervisor is to develop supervisees. Supervisors are responsible to assist supervisees to move to the next level in their development of skills. Supervision is the process of moving a supervisee to the next level of attainment of skills, providing training, mentoring, and modeling competent service delivery. This may involve formal training as well as daily feedback, reshaping, and refining the approach and techniques that a supervisee employs in the delivery of services.

One responsibility of a supervisor is to solve problems. Often supervisees bring problems to supervisors seeking assistance and direction. Simply ignoring the problem or requiring the supervisee to handle it on their own is probably not helpful, however, that doesn't mean that the supervisor takes over responsibility to solve the problem. As part of the supervision process, a supervisor may lead a supervisee to solve her own problems, but solving the problem and resolving the situation in a way that insures the quality of services. Solving problems to insure that high quality services are being provided is an essential part of the role of supervision.

The role of a supervisor, above all else is to prevent harm from occurring to clients. As with any profession, there are some people who probably shouldn't be practicing and may actually do more harm. As a supervisor who is charged with reviewing and monitoring the quality of services, one of the key focuses should be to insure that no clients were harmed in the delivery of a service or treatment. A primary focus of supervision is to be vigilant and aware of a supervisee's issues that could result in clients receiving inadequate service or actually being harmed by the therapeutic process. A supervisor must do everything within their power to insure that their supervisees are not harming clients.

A major aspect of the supervisory relationship that sets it apart from other relationships is evaluation. By its nature, supervision implies that there is going to be an evaluation of the supervisee at some point. At that point, the supervisor shifts into the role of "judge, jury, and executioner." The supervisory relationship is necessarily dominated by a huge power differential. Supervisors have the power in the relationship, to make decisions, prepare evaluations, and write recommendations that can have major ramifications for the supervisee's future. Endorsements for licensure, recommendations for employment, advancement to the next academic skill level are powerful components for a supervisee's future. Supervision is not a collegial relationship, not a relationship with peers, and not a relationship of equals. The power differential will inevitably surface issues of trust, safety, and security. The evaluation and the power differential that is integral to the supervisory relationship are things that have to be dealt with and discussed in supervision. Supervisees need to feel that it's safe to be with you, despite the power differential. Supervisors can make or break careers. This dramatically changes the nature of the relationship.

Originally, the concept of supervision embodied the concept of professional socialization. New professionals needed to develop an understanding of what it meant to be a professional, and this could be accomplished by pairing them with a veteran professional. The pairing or supervisory relationship allowed the supervisor to demonstrate and model for the supervisee how to be a good professional. It was assumed that this socialization process occurred largely through osmosis. How does a professional conduct themselves? What does that look like? How do they talk? How do they dress? What do they act like? The hope was that as a part of a supervisory relationship, the supervisee would acquire professionalism and conduct herself appropriately.

An early experience in socialization for me came from a supervisor who instructed me that "whenever you meet a client in a public situation, you never speak to a client first. They may be with someone that they may not be comfortable explaining how they know you." While that was not learning a major clinical skill, it was a part of that early socialization process. "If you want to be a good professional, you need to learn how to act and conduct yourself appropriately." Handlesman et al. (2005) introduced the concept of *ethical acculturation* i.e. learning the profession's discrete culture, traditions, values and methods. This professional acculturation was viewed as occurring primarily as a natural part of the supervision process.

Supervision versus Consultation

Unfortunately, I think professionals regularly use the term *supervision* casually and inappropriately. A lot of things that we call supervision are not supervision in a strict or legal fashion. Knapp & VandeCreek (2006) made a sharp distinction between supervision and consultation. "Consultation is an arrangement between legal equals in which the consultant provides a service, such as an opinion on a particular case, but the professional receiving the consultation has the right to accept or reject the opinion of the consultant." Supervision and Consultation are fundamentally different. "Supervision occurs when you are overseeing those who cannot legally do what they are doing without your oversight. When supervising others, you have a legal responsibility for their actions. Everything else is consultation and should be labeled as such." APA Trust (2006).

The message is very clear. Be very careful what you label as supervision. If you label it as supervision, and particularly if there are written documents that refer to the activity as supervision, liability and legal responsibility are implied. The Canadian Psychological Association (2000) provided a specific definition that spells out the difference between supervision and consultation for its members: "Consultation occurs between peers or between senior and junior professionals, whereas supervision is provided by an individual who is responsible for the supervisee's work."

If you happen to work in an agency where there's a group of six fully licensed social workers who are providing community mental health services, someone may need to be designated as the person in charge, or the "supervisor." The agency may require that cases are monitored and someone may have to oversee administrative activity and then designate someone as the "supervisor" of that work group. But the legal reality is that those fully licensed social workers can function clinically independent of a "supervisor's" review, monitoring, and oversight. We may refer to that as supervision, but legally it is consultation, unless it can be documented that the supervisor *de facto* assumed supervisory responsibility for their supervisee's actions and responsibility for cases and outcomes.

One issue that clouds our understanding of supervision is the distinction between administrative supervision and clinical supervision, particularly when the same person fills both roles. Activities often called supervision may, in reality, be either consultation or administrative supervision. This point will be discussed in greater detail later in this document. If you are providing clinical supervision, you are responsible for insuring the delivery of high quality services, assisting supervisees to grow and develop, and insuring that clients are not harmed. With those responsibilities, potential liability is inherent.

Conversely, if I am consulting on a case, I may offer my best opinion, but the responsibility for decision making regarding that case remains with you. In a consulting relationship, there is no obligation to follow a consultant's opinion or suggestions. Should you choose to do so, you continue to have the responsibility of the outcome based on your decisions. As a consultant, I have no liability should you choose to follow my advice, or because you choose to ignore it.

Supervisory Competence

Campbell (2000) identified a variety of knowledge, skills, and abilities that are required for competent and effective supervision. She identifies one central component as knowledge of the role and function of a clinical supervisor. This is not a simple role and may require extensive training to become fully competent. Unfortunately, many supervisors are functioning without a clear understanding of what they should be accomplishing or without clearly understanding their role, limitations, and boundaries.

Competent Supervisors must acquire an additional set of conceptual information related to legal, ethical, regulatory issues, licensing, and administrative requirements. Supervisors should have an awareness of, and sensitivity to, the professional and personal nature of supervision and the impact of supervision on the supervisee. Supervisors must also be cognizant of cultural factors, environmental issues, and system issues that impact supervision.

Campbell (2000) further stated that a competent supervisor must have clinical skills in the area that they are supervising. Simply being degreed and licensed does not give a supervisor the competence to supervise any and all services provided by fellow professionals. Since the evaluation component is a key aspect of the supervisory relationship, supervisors must also have some skills in the methods of evaluation.

Supervisors should also have the ability to set goals and objectives and implement a supervision plan. The abilities to avoid or minimize the impact of dual relationships and an understanding of power differentials may be critical factors in insuring a problem-free supervisory experience. And above all else, the ability to fairly and objectively implement evaluation procedures often determines the effectiveness of any supervisory situation.

Haynes et al. (2003) delineated 10 basic components of a competent supervisor.

Basic Components of the Competent Supervisor (Haynes et al, 2003)

> ➤ Trained in supervision and periodically update supervision skills.
> ➤ Trained and experienced in the areas of clinical expertise being supervised.
> ➤ Have effective interpersonal skills (listening, feedback, challenging, setting boundaries, etc.).
> ➤ Aware that supervision is a process and can adapt to individual needs.
> ➤ Able to assume a variety of roles and responsibilities
> ➤ Stay focused on the fact that the primary goal of supervision is to monitor clinical services.
> ➤ Willing and relatively comfortable with serving the evaluative function and providing feedback.
> ➤ Have knowledge of applicable laws, ethics, and professional regulations.
> ➤ Document supervisory activities.
> ➤ Empower a supervisee through teaching, modeling, and problem solving.

The minimal requirements for being a competent supervisor assume a number of skills, experiences, and basic expertise. An essential component is that individual supervisors should be able to demonstrate some level of formal training in supervision and that those skills have been updated through training on a consistent and regular basis. Another basic component is a demonstrated level of clinical skills consistent with the type and nature of the services being provided by those individuals they supervise. Being a licensed supervisor does not confer competence to supervise individuals providing services for which the supervisor has no training, background, experience, or expertise.

The supervisory process is an interaction between two individuals, which by its nature is complicated by the issues of human communication and human interaction. Supervisors should have some demonstrated skills in basic human interaction. Effective interpersonal skills such as listening, being able to provide constructive feedback, creating a challenging learning environment, and setting appropriate boundaries will be critical for effective supervision. A supervisor must be able to have a degree of flexibility and understand that supervision is a process that must be adapted to individual needs and varying skill levels.

Supervisors must be comfortable functioning in a number of different roles and be able to easily move from one role to another. In some situations, supervision requires a nurturing and supportive role and at other times it may demand a harsher and more confrontational role. Above all, supervisors must have a degree of comfort being in an evaluative role and be able to maintain an objectivity that focuses on competence and not their own preferences or idiosyncrasies. The competent and effective supervisor is primarily focused on teaching and developing skills through modeling and appropriate interaction with a supervisee.

Haynes et al. (2003) compiled a list of traits possessed by effective supervisors. What a supervisee considers the qualities of an effective supervisor may vary from one person to another. What might be considered an absolute quality for effective supervision by Supervisee A may be relatively unimportant to Supervisee B. Haynes et al. (2003) felt that an effective supervisor was someone who could clarify expectations and roles, is accessible and available to their supervisees, communicates directly and effectively, and can create a safe learning environment.

On an interpersonal level, a competent supervisor is someone who models appropriate ethical behavior, is personally and professionally mature, has an awareness of personal power and cultural issues, demonstrates empathy, respect, and genuineness, and demonstrates a sense of humor and empathy. Professionally, a competent supervisor possesses good clinical skills, develops clear professional boundaries, respects the supervisee's knowledge, and values supervision as a "protected time."

It is important that a supervisor attempts to create a safe learning environment. The supervisor is responsible for creating an atmosphere where the goal is to learn, the goal is to grow, and the goal is to develop professionally. It is okay to make errors as long as it is a "learning moment."

Telling a practicum one student, who is experiencing their very first practicum, that the only expectation I have for them this first week is that when they go into session they can't fall asleep and they can't fall out of the chair is a humorous attempt at creating a safe learning environment.. It is a conscious attempt to set a tone and an environment where it's okay to be at whatever skill level you are currently. It's okay to learn from mistakes.

Another thing that is very valuable to me personally in a supervisor is having a supervisor with a sense of humor. I want to engage and spend time with an honest to goodness human being. Someone, who can tell a joke and can laugh at my jokes. I want a supervisor who has a little bit of personality as opposed to somebody who is like talking wallpaper.

A competent and ethical supervisor is one who values supervision as a "protected time." Someone who really believes in the importance of supervision and will not place other issues ahead of supervision. Many supervisees report that they never really knew whether supervision was going to occur, because their supervisor could come up with a million different reasons not to have supervision. This sends a message that the supervisor thinks supervision is a low priority. This is in stark contrast to the supervisor who demonstrates that, barring an act of God, supervision will occur as scheduled because it is important. Considering supervision as a "protected time" sends the message that it is important to me as a supervisor to produce good professionals and it's important that supervisees have the opportunity to grow and develop.

The "Best" Supervisors and the "Worst" Supervisors

Martino (2001) surveyed supervisees in an attempt to identify critical factors about a supervisor that can determine the quality of the supervisory experience. The number one factor identified, that is possessed by the "best" supervisors, was clinical knowledge and expertise. A supervisee wants a supervisor who knows what they're doing. A supervisee wants somebody who knows what's going on, who is a true professional and is current and up-to-date. They want a supervisor who is flexible and open to new ideas and willing to attempt something different. While they want someone who is warm and supportive, they also want a supervisor who can critique their work and their skills in order to improve. Supervisees don't want a supervisor who just tells them how wonderful they are. They value an honest, objective critique that they can benefit from and improve their skills to provide better services to their clients.

The "best" supervisors were identified by their interest and commitment to supervision and their capacity for empathy. Those supervisors are individuals who consider transference and countertransference issues and who understand that at the root of all good supervision is a true and honest relationship between the supervisor and the supervisee.

Overwhelmingly, the quality that was most frequently associated with the "worst" supervisor was a lack of interest in supervision or indifference to the professional growth of their supervisees. In some situations, the only reason a supervisor is doing supervision is because their job description requires it. Many are obligated to perform supervision and have no real desire, interest, or passion for developing people. They often just "go through the motions" or approach supervision with a negative attitude. This attitude eventually permeates the learning environment and a supervisee gives up and just goes through the motions themselves.

Another factor that contributes to the "worst" supervisor or a bad supervisory experience is the supervisor who is unavailable, inconsistent, or unreliable. The supervisor who can never be found, the supervisor who can't be contacted, or the supervisor who is always too busy to deal with a supervisee's problems creates an "unsafe learning environment." In this environment, the supervisee feels they are totally on their own, with no support, and having to deal with complex and potentially dangerous situations with "no back-up." They may describe their feelings as being isolated, vulnerable, abandoned, ignored, and left to fend for themselves with issues they may not have the skills or experience to handle.

Punitive supervisors, who view supervision as an opportunity to "whip" supervisees into shape or who are overly harsh or critical also create an unsafe learning environment. These supervisors view their role as waiting for a supervisee to "screw up" and then to drive them into the ground so they never make that mistake again.

Some of these supervisors have been compared to the character "Tigger" in Milne's *Winnie the Pooh*. "Tigger" just bounces merrily along and suddenly, with no apparent rhyme or reason, "pounces" on Christopher Robin. Waiting for the moment that your supervisor will "pounce" does not create a safe learning environment and does not encourage taking reasonable and creative risks.

A supervisor who is unethical does not provide appropriate modeling for supervisees. A supervisor who is uncomfortable assuming a leadership role in a relationship is unlikely to be a good supervisor. Supervision needs to be an experience that has some structure. It needs to be an experience that is directed toward goals based on the particular needs of the supervisee. It is not up to the supervisee to structure the experience, but it is the supervisor who must provide the leadership and direction and appropriately structure the experience. The supervisor must provide structure to the supervision to insure that the goals of monitoring and reviewing activity and professional growth and development are both occurring effectively.

To insure that supervisees receive high quality supervision, Munson (1993) outlined what he called the "*Supervisee's Bill of Rights.*"

Supervisee Bill of Rights (Munson, 1993)

Every supervisee has a right to:

> ➤ A supervisor who supervises consistently and at regular intervals
> ➤ A growth oriented supervisior that respects personal privacy
> ➤ Supervision that is technically sound and theoretically grounded
> ➤ Be evaluated on criteria that are made clear in advance and evaluations that are based on actual observation of performance
> ➤ A supervisor who is adequately skilled in clinical practice and trained in supervision practice

Obviously these are not rights in a legal sense, but are statements as to what the author felt are reasonable expectations that a supervisee is entitled to have during the process of supervision. The purpose of the article is to say that supervisors have a right to expect certain things from their supervisor, including a supervisor who supervises consistently and at regular intervals. A supervisee needs to know that they can count on the fact that at a designated time and place, they will consistently have access to their supervisor and can discuss those problematic situations in their cases.

Supervision is not just an activity to engage in when the supervisor has nothing better to do, but

28

a consistent activity that insures and improves the quality of services being provided. The lack of consistency and regularity is frequently the basis for a licensing board complaint against a supervisor.

A supervisee has a right to a supervisor who is growth oriented and committed to professional growth, but who can also balance the supervisee's right to personal privacy. A reasonable expectation of a supervisee is that they will receive supervision that is technically sound and theoretically grounded with an apparent degree of consistency to one particular approach. A supervisor should have knowledge of clinical issues, a theoretical basis behind what they say, and have some rationale, justification, and research for how they approach supervision.

Supervisees have the right, and in many situations, a legal right, to be evaluated fairly on criteria that are made clear in advance and to be evaluated on actual observation of performance. Lastly, supervisees have a right to a supervisor who is adequately skilled in clinical practice and trained in supervision. In some situations, individuals are appointed to supervisory positions which they haven't been trained or prepared to accept. Placing a supervisee in a situation where they have to rely on someone who has not been adequately trained to perform the duties of supervision is not only frustrating, but can lead to severe negative outcomes for the supervisee and her clients.

For an individual to suddenly assume the role of supervisor without adequate training or sufficient knowledge and information on what it means to be a good supervisor is unfair to the supervisor, supervisee, and clients. Providing individuals who want to become supervisors the opportunity to shadow or sit in with another supervisor, providing basic information about the legal and ethical aspects of supervision, and providing information about different models of supervision would seem to be a minimum level of training required prior to assuming the responsibility of supervision.

Summary

Many misconceptions and misunderstandings exist regarding the concept of clinical supervision. These misconceptions have been perpetuated by inadequately trained individuals providing supervision. Perhaps the biggest misconception is that simply being a competent therapist or practitioner automatically makes an individual a competent supervisor. Another misconception is that supervision is purely about case review. While this is important, it is only one aspect of supervision. Another major responsibility of supervision is quality control of services and ensuring that clients are not harmed. Training and socialization are also major components of the supervisory process.

A distinction must be made between the process of supervision and consultation. Supervision implies that the supervisor has legal responsibility for the actions and decisions of their supervisees; whereas, consultation is a process of collaboration between peers or a senior and junior professional and no legal responsibility occurs or is implied.

Many professions have wrestled with the concept of supervisory competence and when, how, and where does competent supervision occur. Formal training is a major assumption of supervisory competence, yet many supervisors have had limited or no formal training in, or understanding of, the supervisory process and dynamic.

Studies have indicated that some qualities that the "best" supervisors have include: clinical

31

knowledge, flexibility, the ability to be supportive, a dedication to professional development, an awareness of transference issues, and adherence to ethical practices. "Worst" supervisors often lack interest in professional development, are unavailable, inflexible, have limited clinical knowledge, are punitive, and lack the ability to provide a structure in which effective supervision can occur.

A supervisees has a right to reasonably expect supervision at regular intervals, a growth oriented supervisor, a supervisor who is technically and theoretically grounded. They also should be able to expect to be evaluated fairly, on criteria made clear in advance, and based on actual performance.

CHAPTER TWO

Models of Clinical Supervision

Administrative Supervision vs. Clinical Supervision

In order to be a competent and effective supervisor, one key distinction that has to be made is to determine the type of supervision being provided. In many situations, particularly individuals who are employed by nonprofit organizations or governmental agencies, supervisors are required to provide both administrative and clinical supervision. Simultaneously having both administrative supervisory responsibilities as well as clinical supervisory responsibilities places a supervisor in a particularly difficult situation. Providing both types of supervision creates a dual relationship. It is not necessarily unethical, but the dual relationship is something that has to be managed very carefully.

Administrative supervision and clinical supervision have different purposes. They typically utilize different models and methods and have different goals. There are completely different sets of rules, operations, and expectations depending on whether you are doing administrative supervision or clinical supervision. In many situations the rules are in opposition or conflicting and create a conflict of interest.

Supervisors who are performing administrative supervision have a fiduciary responsibility to whatever entity, agency, foundation, or tax base is funding the organization. The fiduciary responsibility to carry out the expectations and contractual obligations of the funding source carries its own set of ethical and legal obligations. As an administrative supervisor, there is an obligation to use those resources and those funds appropriately and effectively for the purpose intended. Supervisees and other staff are one of those resources that you are entrusted with to provide services. In addition, you clearly have a responsibility to the people providing the services.

As a result of the fiduciary responsibility, an administrative supervisor must frequently operate from a business model. In fact, a lot of administrative supervisors may have advanced training in business courses or are working toward their MBA. Administrative supervisors approach problems from a business perspective, i.e., getting the most out of personnel, rather than what is in the supervisee's best interest, growth, or development.

As a clinical supervisor, it is important to insure that the supervisee has a caseload that is manageable, and also allows the supervisee to provide quality services and concurrently promotes the development of new skills in a supervisee. As an administrative supervisor, the supervisor has to insure that all cases are covered. If a staff member suddenly develops a serious illness, the existing cases will need to be covered. The supervisor may have to reassign a large number of cases to a supervisee which they know will compromise the quality of a supervisee's casework, does not allow for the development of new skills, and may actually be beyond the supervisee's abilities. The supervisor may know that the decision to reassign cases does not help the supervisee to grow clinically, but as an administrative supervisor, operating from a business model, the supervisor's role and fiduciary responsibility are to "keep the doors open."

Administrative supervision is about keeping the organization functioning. The administrative supervisor's first concern is the health and survival of the organization. As a result, the administrative supervisor has to get involved with issues of hiring, promotions, raises, productivity, caseload size, cost per service, reimbursement rates, etc. These are issues that administrative supervisors struggle with from a pure business perspective. Administrative supervisors may be forced to make decisions primarily on the basis of what is good for the system and secondarily what is in the best interest of clients and supervisees.

An administrative supervisor has to be concerned with federal, state, and local labor laws, EEOC guidelines, and contract regulations. In some situations an administrative supervisor must operate within a union environment and the restrictions of a union contract. Administrative supervisors have to make decisions about supervisees regarding merit raises, disciplinary actions, or placing a supervisee on probation or a work plan. These activities may be in direct conflict with the clinical supervisor's focus on client services and the supervisee's growth and development.

Clinical supervision operates from a non-business model. Clinical supervisors are more focused on developing their supervisee's skills. Increasing the supervisee's competency, knowledge about functioning in an ethical fashion, and professional development in order to provide high quality services to clients are the points of emphasis. The feedback and critique that are given to a supervisee are directed toward improving service delivery, not on whether or not the supervisee receives a raise.

Critique is not discipline, but an analysis of actions and decisions to determine if other actions or decisions would have been more beneficial for the client. Part of the role of clinical supervisor is to interpret the legal restrictions, licensing mandates, and the Ethics Code, not as a business manager, but as a well-versed professional. Evaluation by a clinical supervisor is going to be from the perspective of providing ongoing feedback about skills and service delivery. Every clinical supervision session should have some element of providing feedback and evaluation as opposed to an annual performance appraisal which may be more characteristic of administrative supervision.

Bernard & Goodyear (2009) stated "The clinical supervisor has a dual investment in the quality of services and professional development; whereas, the administrative supervisor focuses on communication, protocol, personnel policy, and fiscal issues." This, at times, can produce conflict, as several competing, but legitimate sets of needs are operating simultaneously. The client has legitimate needs; the supervisee has legitimate needs; the supervisor has legitimate needs; and the organization has legitimate needs. All these legitimate sets of needs will undoubtedly conflict at times and one set of needs must be weighed against another in decision making.

Understanding and managing the distinction between administrative and clinical supervision is important enough that the Canadian Psychological Association (2009) has defined supervision as occurring on two levels: Developmental (Clinical) and Administrative. Developmental supervision has as its "primary objective facilitating skill development through education/training/mentoring. The essential administrative function is described as "management that emphasizes quality control." Recognizing the dual relationship and the conflicting needs is the first step in ethically managing many difficult situations.

Models of Supervision

A generally held assumption regarding competent supervision is that there is an underlying philosophy, a set of principles, and defined techniques that guide this activity called supervision. In the literature it is frequently referred to as having a Model of Supervision. Unfortunately, if you ask most supervisors, "What is your Model of Supervision?" you may receive blank stares, stuttering, or a rambling set a verbiage that provides little coherence or understanding. Having a model of supervision, being able to discuss your model intelligently, and being able to demonstrate some level of training in a particular model can be a way of establishing *prima facie* competence in supervision and supervisory activities.

In any activity, the inability to demonstrate competency presents the potential for liability. The ability to identify a particular model of supervision and training in that model of supervision puts you in a more comfortable position if you are seated in the witness stand, being deposed, or have been called before the licensing board. Unfortunately, many supervisors have received little formal training in supervision and are erroneously trying to supervise in the ways that they were supervised. This is sometimes referred to as the "No-Model."

"No model" Model of Supervision

The "No-Model" Model of supervision is typically another way of saying, "I supervise the same way my supervisors supervised me." Whatever was good in my experience as a supervisee, I'm replicating; whatever was bad in that experience, I'm also replicating. The No-Model Model ensures that you have no theoretical or evidentiary basis for what you are doing and are more likely to flounder due to a lack of theory, research, and direction. In addition to lacking direction, purpose and documented effectiveness, the No-Model probably replicates the same mistake your supervisor made, while adding in a few of your own mistakes.

Apprentice-Master Model

Another ineffective model of supervision is the Apprentice-Master Model. This model dates back to at least the Middle Ages, and possibly beyond. An individual, new to a profession or wishing to learn a profession, would apprentice themselves to a master craftsman. This model has an assumption that the supervisee knows very little, has very few skills, and is generally incompetent to practice the profession. This model is one that clearly emphasizes the power differential and may even encourage the supervisor to rely on and reinforce the feeling of incompetence on the part of the supervisee. An assumption is made that if the supervisee simply "hangs out" with a skilled professional long enough and under close observation, by the process of osmosis, the supervisee will magically develop the skills of being the good clinician. This assumption in many instances turned out to be false.

The Expert Model

A model that continues to be practiced today which creates some questionable practices and is questionably effective is the Expert Model. This model is frequently practiced in medical settings as evidenced by Grand Rounds. It starts with a number of questionable assumptions, which may become problematic in the supervision process. Supervision is a "top-down" model with the expert holding all the power and the ability to be very punitive. This often does not create a very safe learning environment and many supervisees may resort to "hiding their mistakes" rather than suffer ridicule or a negative evaluation from the expert. The "right-wrong" atmosphere implies that the supervisee has little to offer and due to their incompetence needs to be closely directed and monitored. This model does not sit well with experienced clinicians who feel like they are already competent, but are looking for supervision to refine their existing skills.

The One-Size-Fits-All Model

Another model of supervision that has not been demonstrated to be particularly effective is the One-Size-Fits-All Model. The supervisor approaches all supervisees exactly the same way despite their level of professional development or their individual growth needs. Supervision should look and feel different with the relatively inexperienced person versus the interaction with an experienced veteran where the focus is polishing skills. The supervisor who doesn't make that kind of distinction operates in a One-Size-Fits-All Model. This approach insures that neither the experienced nor inexperienced supervisee's needs are met as supervision is not tailored to meet the needs of the supervisee.

If an individual is a practicum one student, a number of issues may need to be addressed that a supervisor doesn't have to deal with in an individual who has 15 or 20 years of experience. If you watched tapes of supervision of those two individuals, the method and techniques should be readily distinguishable. The supervisor must recognize that there are two different skill sets that are being addressed and that supervision and supervision style needs to fit the needs and experience level of the supervisee.

The Therapist-As-Patient Model

The Therapist-As-Patient Model was widely used in the 70s and 80s. Part of the role of the supervisor was to "therapize" the supervisee and identify their hidden idiosyncrasies, their psychopathology, and their Axis II Disorders. Once identified, the role of the supervisor was to purge them of their individual issues. The assumption was that the supervisee's issues may be getting in the way of their being a good therapist. While this may have produced generations of emotionally healthy therapists, it did not impart a lot of concrete skills. The focus unfortunately became assisting the supervisee with personal issues, rather than assisting the supervisee to serve the client effectively and safely.

The Parallel Process Model

An effective model of supervision is the Parallel Process Model. The basic assumption is that the supervisee's experience with clients will also be reflected in the supervisee's relationship with the supervisor and vice versa (Storm and Todd, 1997; Frawley-O'Dea & Sarnat, 2001; and Yorke, 2005). Supervision looks at both relationships with an assumption that relationships on any given level influence those on another level. Whatever is going on between the client and the supervisee will be reflected in the relationship between the supervisee and supervisor. This isomorphic, systemic approach assumes that whatever dynamic exists between the supervisee and her clients, the same dynamic exists in supervision.

The supervisor can use the dynamics observed in her supervisee's cases to talk about the dynamic of what's going on in supervision and how that might be preventing supervision from being effective. The flip side is, that whatever issues the supervisee and the supervisor have going on (i.e. difficulty handling conflictual situations), there is a significant probability those issues are showing up in therapy. This systemic approach says, let's look at how you are with clients and look at the supervisory relationship and recognize that there are parallel processes in existence.

The Interactional Model/ Relationship Model

The Interactional Model and Relationship Model both approach supervision by looking at the quality of the relationship between the supervisor and supervisee. One of the early pioneers in this area was Bordin (1983) who espoused the concept of the *Supervisory Working Alliance*. The Supervisory Working Alliance involved creating a collaborative relationship between the supervisor and supervisee with agreed goals and objectives and a strong emotional bond of caring, trust, and respect.

Supervision was seen as a way of creating a reciprocal relationship based on mutuality of needs. Having those needs met in the supervisory relationship would result in needs being met in the client relationship (Shulman, 1993). The assumption was that when the supervisory relationship is going well and meeting the supervisee's needs, clients will receive excellent service. The supervisory relationship is the medium by which supervision occurs and many experienced supervisees view the supervisory relationship as the most important aspect of high quality supervision. Kaiser (1997) identified the four key elements of an effective supervisory relationship: accountability, personal awareness, trust and power, and use of authority.

The Developmental Model

The Developmental Models consist of a number of approaches, including the *Supervisor Complexity Model* Watkins (1997) and Inman and Ladany (2008), the *Integrated Developmental Model* as discussed by Stoltenberg and McNeil (1998, 2009) and the *Discrimination Model* as developed by Bernard (1997). The consistent factor that all three have in common is the premise that not everyone should be supervised the same way. Through an assessment process, the supervisor identifies each supervisee's skills and then supervises them in a fashion that helps the supervisee attain the next level of their development.

The supervision required to achieve that next developmental level would be a very different experience for a novice therapist than it would be for a long-term veteran with 15 years of experience. The level of the supervisee's skills should be very apparent based on the manner in which a supervisor is interacting with a supervisee. In all Developmental Models, the supervisor will be called upon to individualize supervision plans and methods and to tailor supervision to the developmental needs of the supervisee. Developmental Models are based on the premise that the supervisor, supervisee, and supervisory relationship change over time consistent with the growth and development of the supervisee.

The Holistic Model

The Holistic Model was developed by Campbell (2000 & 2006) and focuses on providing an atmosphere of safety, trust, and learning. The Holistic Model also looks at the idea of parallel processes, but a major focus of the holistic model is achieved by building on the strengths of the individual supervisee, rather than focusing on problems or deficits. "Catch a supervisee doing something right." While the supervisor is still concerned about errors, mistakes, or sub-par services, the focus is on growth and development.

The supervisor's personal goal is to be able to help the supervisee develop. The supervisor desires to identify the things that the supervisee is naturally good at and then develop those abilities so that they can be used therapeutically in the room with clients. If a supervisee is a "natural joiner," that is, they have never met a stranger and can talk easily to almost everyone, develop that ability to relate to people in a way that it enhances the delivery of services.

Summary

A distinction must be made between administrative supervision and clinical supervision. Administrative supervision involves a fiduciary responsibility to the organization or funding source and may require decisions and judgments that are in the interest of the organization rather than in the interest of the individual supervisee. Administrative supervision operates from a business model and is focused on keeping the organization solvent and functioning. Issues of efficiency and effectiveness may be emphasized over professional or personal development.

Clinical supervision operates from a "non-business" model and is more concerned about professional development and training. Professional development is emphasized to increase competent service delivery and insure that clients receive ethical services. Unfortunately, many supervisors operate from an absence of any theory or unified concept of the supervisory process. Clinical supervision can operate effectively and competently under a number of theoretical models including the: Parallel Process Model, Interactional Model, Relationship Model, Developmental Model, Developmental Models, and a Holistic Model.

Whatever model that a supervisor may choose to employ, an overarching concern that applies equally to all models is the concept of attempting to create a non-hostile and safe learning environment. Campbell (2006) calls this the key to any kind of effective supervision and identifies a number of critical components that go into creating an atmosphere where supervisees feel safe and trusted. However, if supervisees don't feel safe, they will distort the process of supervision to protect themselves. Supervisees may even go to the extent of lying, or couching the truth in a less negative fashion to protect themselves from a hostile supervisory environment. Creating a safe learning environment can be accomplished if the supervisor is genuine and respectful, is available, consistent, and reliable. The supervisor can attempt to create an environment that is as positive as possible and not overly focused on the negative.

Finally, the supervisor's most effective tool toward creating a non-hostile environment is the ability to laugh and have a sense of humor. When supervision becomes a painful experience that supervisees come to dread and attempt to avoid, learning and skill development will cease.

CHAPTER THREE

Supervisory Formats and Techniques

Individual Supervision

A number of different processes or formats are commonly employed in supervision. Individual supervision is the most common format and traditionally dates back to Freud or beyond. This is the format for supervision which is typically required by licensing boards and training programs. It characteristically consists of face-to-face review of case records at a minimum, but may also include other strategies in the context of individual consultation.

One obvious advantage is that in individual, one-on-one supervision the supervisee receives individualized attention. There are fewer opportunities for embarrassment and the safer environment may encourage reasonable risk taking and growth. Individual supervision also allows the supervisor to tailor the supervisory approach to the needs, experience level, and developmental stage of the supervisee. Finally, the supervisee does not have to compete with others to get the feedback and direction that they may need from their supervisor.

Some obvious disadvantages might include an inaccurate or preconceived impression of the superviseee, supervisor bias or prejudices, and the opportunity for supervisee deception in supervision. Typically, individual supervision relies heavily on the self-report of the supervisee and there is always the opportunity for conscious or unconscious deception. If the supervisor relies solely of a self-report format, they may have very limited or skewed information about what is actually going on in an individual case.

Exclusive reliance on self-report in supervision, i.e. "tell me about your cases," limits the supervisor's knowledge of what the supervisee's cases are really like. Even if the supervisee is not consciously trying to deceive, the supervisor is relying on information that has been filtered through the supervisee's perceptions. There is a real danger that the information is presented in a way that may or may not be an accurate reflection of the status of their cases. Supervisory oversight may be severely limited.

Group Supervision

While individual supervision is probably the most commonly utilized approach, group supervision is also frequently employed and has a number of advantages and disadvantages. An obvious advantage with group supervision is that a number of people can receive supervision at the same time, increasing cost-effectiveness. Increasing the number of ideas and perspectives by having additional people involved in the process can also be advantageous.

I have found this to be particularly effective with students who are in supervision for an assessment practicum. Reviewing testing data, technical testing aspects, and test protocols with an individual can become a very tedious and boring task for both the supervisor and supervisee. However, by having a number of students in the room at the same time reviewing their testing, the other students may be exposed to a particular technical piece of information which may not come up in individual supervision. There is a real opportunity for cross-fertilization to occur by having students view and review someone else's testing protocols.

Many of the same problems and issues that occur in doing group therapy will also be present in group supervision. As in group therapy, confidentiality issues, trust issues, and creating a sense of safety are primary and have to be dealt with effectively in group supervision. While doing group supervision, the group leader or supervisor is responsible for managing the dynamic of the group. This might include managing the supervisee that attempts to dominate the whole session, or the supervisee who is reluctant to talk or engage in the process.

The composition of the group in terms of size, skill level, and client populations must be thoughtfully considered and regulated. The effectiveness of group supervision is going to depend on the supervisor's skills as a group leader and skills at managing group dynamics. There are some supervisors who are particularly skilled at doing groups, while other supervisors are much more effective in a one-on-one environment. Group supervision can also be very valuable as an adjunct or supplement to individual supervision.

Team Supervision

Rarely, but in some agencies, supervision may be provided by a team of supervisors, particularly if the supervisee is working in a number of different program areas within an organization. What might occur in some organizations, is that a supervisee leads client groups in an inpatient setting and is supervised by a psychiatrist. If they also provide outpatient services or aftercare, for that service, they might be being supervised by a psychologist, social worker, or marriage and family therapist. If they also work in a specialized area such as eating disorders, they might be being supervised by yet another supervisor.

Rather than having three different supervisors and the confusion that will inevitably occur, team supervision is occasionally used as an effective option. Team supervision is an activity where all the individual supervisors meet concurrently with the supervisee. One obvious advantage is that the supervisee is provided a unique opportunity to learn from three diverse professionals, with three singular theoretical backgrounds, and with three dissimilar experience sets.

While it can be somewhat intimidating if you're the supervisee who is sitting down once a week with three professionals who are ultimately your bosses, an experience of team supervision, done well, can be enormously beneficial. The supervisee is exposed to the approach which a supervisor would take as a clinical psychologist and may also experience the approach that a family therapist might take, as well as being exposed to the approach that a psychiatrist might take. Hopefully, in the process, the supervisee recognizes that there are multiple, legitimate ways of conceptualizing a case. The supervisee can develop an understanding and appreciation that varying legitimate perspectives may result in different, but equally beneficial interventions.

A danger with team supervision is that some supervisees are very good at playing the game of "let the supervisors fight it out," or in more clinical terms, triangulation. The time commitment of multiple professionals to the supervisory process and managing the dynamic of the supervision team are drawbacks to a team supervision approach. Many supervisees have reported that team supervision is a great learning tool, and they have come to value the varying perspectives that they are exposed to by team supervision. Team supervision can also be useful for supervisors in dealing with problematic supervisees or supervisor/supervisee conflict situations, or dual relationships.

Peer Supervision (Consultation)

Another method of supervision, that probably should not be called supervision in the fullest sense of the word, is peer supervision (consultation). A more appropriate designation from a legal standpoint may be to refer to it as peer consultation. Peer supervision (consultation) provides an opportunity for supervisees to work together, to offer mutual support, and to exchange ideas about cases. Peer consultation probably is not sufficient to serve as the only supervision that an individual is receiving, but may be a great adjunct to individual supervision. Peer consultation normally works best when individuals have similar levels of training, background, and types of cases.

Peer consultation is very useful and should be encouraged at all levels of training, licensure or experience. It is very doubtful that any legal liability occurs for group members with peer consultation, but a practitioner who regularly consults with peers actually enhances making the case that they are a competent provider. It is very unlikely that any court or licensing board would attempt to hold someone liable who consulted informally on a case. If the consultant was being paid for advice, then there may be more opportunities to make an argument that the consultant has some potential liability.

Case Consultation

Some agencies and organizations may require independently licensed practitioners to be "supervised." Again, this should be more appropriately labeled as case consultation, coordination, administrative supervision, or professional development. Case consultation limits liability on the part of the "supervisor/case consultant." The advantage of professionals consulting with others on cases is that it forces practitioners to organize information, conceptualize problems, make assessments, and decide on interventions in a more organized fashion.

Consulting may also encourage the consultee to consider the larger context and ethical issues in a particular case. Disadvantages include the fact that the consultant has very limited information on which to suggest interventions, and the information the consultant is utilizing depends on the conceptual and observational abilities of the supervisee.

Live Supervision

There are many methods of doing live supervision, i.e. a supervisor is actually viewing the services as they are being provided. Some of these methods of live supervision are purely observational such as the supervisor sitting in on sessions, viewing the session through a one-way mirror, watching a session transpire through closed circuit television, on-line video conferencing, or audio or video taping.

The advantages are that live supervision provides the supervisor the opportunity to have first-hand knowledge of the services being provided. This is an added strategy to ensure that quality services are occurring. Corrective or supportive feedback can be provided regarding very specific aspects of the service delivery. This should allow the supervisee to adjust their style and techniques based on this feedback.

Other types of live supervision techniques are more focused on interactional methods. With these approaches, critique and the opportunity for correction take place in live time. A supervisor who "sits in" on a session may become very active in the therapeutic process as a way of demonstrating or modeling, or even actually engaging in co-therapy. Less invasive techniques, for both the client and the supervisee, may include "buzzing in" or "calling in," or calling the supervisee out of the session into the hallway with specific suggestions or ideas. Using the "bug-in-the-ear" technology to provide the supervisee with an ongoing stream of critique, suggestions, and support has also been demonstrated to be an effective learning tool.

The ability to review video recordings of sessions or audio recorded versions of sessions takes supervision from the level of relying on the self-report of supervisors to the concrete observation of what goes on in sessions. A supervisor who relies on their supervisee for information about cases is more vulnerable to criticism about not effectively controlling the quality of services. A supervisee may report that everything is fine and remarkable progress is being made by a particular client. However, when the supervisor observes first-hand what is going on, a very different picture emerges and there may be real concerns about the quality of services being delivered.

Reviewing recorded sessions with a supervisee promotes self-awareness and self-correction. Obviously, informed consent must be obtained from the client and should include how the recording will be used, who will see it or hear it, if it will be available in staffing or seminars. The informed consent should also specify how the recording will be physically safeguarded, and a timetable for retention and destruction of the media.

Policies and procedures should be written and in place to deal with the real life issues of consent, access, privacy, and the possibility of media being subpoenaed by a court. Storage issues, physical security, access issues, and the length of time media is stored must be carefully considered. Sessions stored on tape, or digitally, provide both a method of preventing liability as well as documentation of liability depending on the actual content of the session.

Two examples illustrate the need to think through procedures for recording sessions and safeguarding the information. At Agency X, supervisees were required to videotape all sessions. In the days of VHS, supervisees routinely put a tape in the wall mounted camera at the beginning of the day and hit the record button. This worked rather well until a man revealed in the session that he was molesting his granddaughter. A relatively new therapist panicked and left the room to find a supervisor. When the supervisee came back, the client was gone, as well as the camera and the tape. Unfortunately, the tape had four other clients' sessions on it. A long process ensued, involving lawyers, police, and court orders, in order to get the tape returned, insuring other clients' privacy.

Another supervisee made a DVD recording of sessions at Agency Y. Supervision was being provided off-site. The supervisee stored the DVD in his briefcase and drove to supervision, stopping on the way to get some lunch. While he was in the restaurant, his car, along with the briefcase, and the DVD, was stolen. The car was ultimately recovered, but the briefcase and DVD were never found. Letters had to be sent to clients, whose sessions were on the DVD, informing them about the breach of security, creating potential liability for the agency and supervisee.

Computerized (On-line) Supervision

Advances in technology may make supervision appear very differently in the future. Computer technology presents an unlimited set of confidentiality issues as well as unlimited opportunities for supervisory innovation. With new possibilities comes the potential for additional issues and problems. The internet and teleconferencing provide an opportunity for increased efficiency, particularly in situations that might involve travel over significant distances.

In some situations licensing board and regulatory bodies may not recognize computerized supervision as meeting the requirement for once a week face-to-face supervision. Some Boards of Psychology have authorized the utilization of supervision over the internet "on a limited basis and under special circumstances." Other professional organizations are beginning to recognize this issue and the trends toward this type of supervision by adopting their own standards. AAPC (2009) states "distance supervision meets the requirement for live supervision if it is conducted in 'real time,' that is, telephone conversation, video-teleconference, or live internet chat technology."

Issues of computer security, electronic transmission of protected health information, storage of data and information, off-site storage complicate supervision online using the internet. Contracting for teleconferencing services with vendors and how these providers will handle the information may complicate the utilization of computerized supervision, but will certainly not prevent it from being widely used in the future.

Supervision over the phone and supervision via e-mail also create their own unique situations. These strategies limit full access to communication cues such as non-verbals and body language. Online supervision eliminates geography and provides opportunities for supervisees to be supervised by masters in the field. This is a particularly attractive option for veteran clinicians who are looking to move their skills to another level, but might not have access to that expertise in their local community.

Didactic Supervision

Unfortunately, as the concept and value of supervision have developed over time, the pendulum may have swung over the years to the point that supervision has become overly focused on case review and improving techniques. Supervisors may be missing out on opportunities for professional growth and facilitating the professional socialization of the supervisee. Supervisors may be so focused on quality review and case strategies that they ignore growth and development opportunities.

Most supervisors have had extensive experience and have become very skilled in service provision. Over the years, supervisors may have "learned some stuff." It would be unfortunate if there was not a conscious attempt to "pass along some of that stuff." Actually teaching a particular set of skills, imparting a body of knowledge, or sharing some hard earned professional insights are legitimate activities for supervision.

Having a list of professional topics that a supervisor can surface when there are a few minutes left in supervision may be a very valuable component of supervision. Introducing topics such as: intervention techniques, developing self-awareness, assessment and diagnostic issues, cultural differences, documentation, practicing from a theoretical perspective, practicing within one's competence, setting boundaries with clients, practicing ethically, professionalism, and using community resources may add a needed richness and wealth to the supervisory experience. It would be a mistake to ignore cases and quality control and make supervision solely a teaching, lecturing experience, but some imparting of information can enhance the supervisory experience.

Summary

Clinical supervision may be practiced under a number of models, many of which may include similar formats or techniques. Individual supervision, one-on-one interaction between a supervisor and supervisee is perhaps the most frequently used format and provides the advantages of individualization, a safe learning environment, and tailoring the supervisory sessions to the developmental level and needs of the individual supervisee.

Disadvantages include problematic dynamics between a supervisor and supervisee, an over reliance on self-report, and limited first-hand knowledge of the supervisee's work.

Another common supervisory format is group supervision. It is a much more efficient and cost-effective alternative to individual supervision provides multiple perspectives, and increases the opportunity for cross-fertilization of ideas. Group supervision is a natural opportunity for supervisees to provide each other with mutual support; however, many of the same issues that are problematic in group therapy are prevalent in group supervision. These include managing the group dynamic, domination of the supervision by one or two individuals, a mismatch of individuals of different experience and skill levels, and the skill of the supervisor at managing group interaction. In some situations, group supervision can be a very beneficial adjunct to relying primarily on individual supervision.

Team supervision occurs in some setting where a supervisee has multiple supervisors and rather than meet individually with each supervisor, supervision occurs by a team of supervisors. This provides an opportunity to review cases from multiple perspectives and provides professional modeling of appropriate professional interaction. Unfortunately, it is very costly supervision that also provides an opportunity for the supervisee to triangulate the supervisors.

Peer supervision is actually a misnomer which should be labeled as peer consultation or peer review, as supervision cannot legally occur between peers. Peer consultation is a great opportunity for developing skills, providing and obtaining professional support, and exploring alternative strategies that might be utilized. Case consultation in not actual supervision, but is a strategy for professional development and creative problem solving. Case consultation can be very effective in improving service delivery and receiving feedback regarding service provision.

Live supervision is extremely effective at providing a supervisor with firsthand knowledge of the supervisee's actual skills at service delivery. It can provide the supervisee with immediate feedback, the opportunity to make corrections, and to attempt new avenues of service delivery. Learning occurs in the here and now and is more experiential than simple case reporting. In situations where actual service observation cannot occur, recording sessions allows the supervisor a closer and more intimate knowledge of service provision and allows for self-observation by the supervisee. When utilizing recordings for supervision, care must be taken to insure confidentiality, security of the data, and the ultimate disposition of the materials. Policies and procedures must be in place and part of the supervisory responsibility is to insure that these are followed.

The expansion of technology provides for increased opportunities and creative formats for supervision, but also creates a number of concerns that must be addressed. Computerized or on-line supervision is increasingly being used for efficiency, as well as providing for opportunities for supervision by renowned experts who are physically in a different location. While this provides extremely creative ways in which supervision can occur, confidentiality of the communications, storage issues, going to a two dimension interaction, miscommunication, and cross state licensing issues are areas that need further exploration and consideration.

Finally, while supervision is not didactic teaching, supervision should include informal as well as formal opportunities for supervisors to share their knowledge and experience with supervisees. Using a part of the supervision for discussion of professional topics and ethical issues is extremely important.

CHAPTER FOUR

Ethical Issues in Supervision

When considering ethical issues regarding supervision, a distinction must be made between supervising ethically and supervising legally. If a supervisor is supervising in a legal fashion, complying with all state, federal, and local statutes and regulations, she still may not be supervising in an ethical fashion given the ethics codes of her particular profession.

Ethics codes often demand more from professionals than simple adherence to statutes and regulations. For example, if supervision meets all the statutory and regulatory responsibilities, but there is not a written supervisory agreement, the supervisor may be in violation of their particular code of ethics. While the supervisor is certainly supervising in a legal fashion they may not be supervising in an ethical fashion, and are clearly acting unethically.

If a supervisor is supervising in an ethical fashion, adhering to all the mandates and criteria spelled out in the ethics code of their profession, that does not necessarily mean that they are supervising in a legal fashion. This situation is less likely to occur, as some ethics codes require compliance with all federal state and local rules and regulations. It is assumed that all supervisors want to conduct themselves in an ethical fashion; however, the requirements for ethical supervision are much less specific and open to a variety of interpretations.

Campbell (2006) identified what she believes to be Ten Activities Required for Ethical Supervision.

> Be trained; be competent
> Orient supervisees
> Informed Consent Agreement
> Know current ethical codes
> Have goals for supervision
> Create plans and structure for supervision
> Plan for evaluation criteria and methods
> Dialogue about dual relationships and multicultural issues (Lowe, 2010)
> Document, document, document, document..............
> Regular supervision of supervision, not crisis consultation

One basic requirement for being an ethical supervisor is to be trained in supervision and competent to conduct the activities and responsibilities of a supervisor. In many situations, particularly in public agencies, individuals are often pushed into supervisory positions without any formal preparation or additional training. An individual may be a great clinician, but that does not guarantee that they will be a good supervisor. In fact, many individuals who are skilled clinicians turn out to be lousy supervisors. Without some degree of formalized training, it is highly unlikely that a supervisor can be competently performing their duties and thereby may be acting unethically. Many ethical codes specifically provide for, and certainly the professional literature regarding supervision, talks about the need for meeting certain basic qualifications in order to be considered a supervisor.

Another hallmark of an ethical supervisor might be having informed consent agreements between the client and the supervisee, and the supervisee and the supervisor. Acting without a clearly defined set of parameters regarding supervision, as would be spelled out in an informed consent agreement, places both the supervisor and the supervisee in a precarious situation. Failure to obtain informed consent from supervisees may violate the Standard of Care for Supervision and therefore, be unethical. An informed consent agreement tells supervisees where the out of bounds markers are and the rules and limits for providing services while under direct supervision. An informed consent agreement spells out the nature of the relationship and allows the supervisee to consent fully to the specific activities of supervision.

An ethical supervisor is one who is current with, and highly aware of, the ethical code of their particular profession. Without an up-to-date awareness of the existing ethics codes, it may be very difficult, if not impossible for a supervisor to model appropriate ethical behavior. Supervisees frequently will approach supervisors with questions regarding the ethical provision of services. Supervisees have a legitimate right to expect an informed answer, based on the current ethics codes of their particular profession. To be unaware of or ill-informed about ethical issues would make supervision that conforms to an appropriate standard of care difficult, if not impossible.

Supervising ethically will require the supervisor to provide an appropriate format and structure in which effective supervision can take place. Establishing goals and objectives for supervision and developing a reasonable plan to achieve those goals is an integral part of effectively and ethically supervising. It is not the supervisee's responsibility to create an atmosphere and structure where the quality of casework is monitored, growth and development occur, and clients are prevented from being harmed. Establishing a system of documentation of supervisory activities that insures a high quality of services and provides both a record and a direction for future efforts is part of being an ethical supervisor.

Supervisees have a right to know the criteria on which they are being evaluated. Supervising ethically may mean the supervisor makes considerable efforts to ensure that there are no surprises or misunderstandings. Letting supervisees know in advance what is expected of them and what is required of them can go a long way toward preventing dissatisfaction or disagreements regarding performance evaluation. An ethical supervisor does not spring surprises or traps for a supervise. Evaluation criteria are made known well in advance and are made as clear as humanly possible.

An ethical supervisor must not be afraid to engage in conversations regarding dual relationships or multicultural issues. Avoiding conversations about sensitive issues may create significant difficulties in supervision. A real danger for a supervisor is the failure to recognize that their work as a supervisor also needs to be reviewed to ensure quality of care, growth and development, and prevent harm from occurring to supervisees. Some veteran supervisors feel that they are overwhelmingly competent and require little or no oversight. This may put them in the position of not meeting an individual supervisee's needs and requirements. Ongoing consultation regarding supervision, or supervision of supervision, is a responsible way to ensure that supervisors are continuing to be effective and ethical. Assuming that a number of years as a supervisor automatically ensures ethical and competent supervision can be a recipe for disaster.

One of the significant issues with attempting to be an ethical supervisor is that, in many instances, ethical codes do not provide a clear answer or direction as to how supervisory activities are to be conducted. The nature of ethics prohibits or prevents an ethics code from being developed that is so detailed that it will cover every situation and every circumstance. There are some situations that no one could ever foresee or imagine, let alone develop a specific ethical standard to address.

At best, ethical codes almost universally start with the premise of some basic core principles that the profession aspires to and then attempts to develop a structure and guidelines based on those core principles. Ethics codes may make some direct statements regarding fairly commonly observed situations, but these core principles must then be applied specifically to each supervisory relationship and situation. Each profession's code of ethics is a statement of beliefs and general principles that fellow professionals have developed as a consensus and have agreed upon.

Core Ethical Principles	
APA (2002)	**NASW (2008)**
Beneficence/Nonmaleficence	Service
Fidelity/Responsibility	Social Justice
Integrity	Integrity
Justice	Dignity/Worth of Person
Respect for Human Rights	Competence
Importance of Human Relations	Dignity

Pope and Vasquez (1998) reviewed disciplinary actions by state boards of psychology over a 15 year period. The most frequent reason for ethical complaints filed with the state board of psychology was sexual violations or dual relationship issues. These accounted for almost

35% of all ethics complaints, followed by unprofessional, unethical, negligent practice (28.6%), fraud (9.5%), and convictions of crimes (8.6%). The fifth most frequent reason for complaint being filed with the state licensing board was for improper or inadequate supervision (4.9%).

Almost all supervisors view themselves as supervising in an ethical fashion; however, this does not guarantee that supervisees actually perceive supervisors as being ethical.. Ladany et al. (1999) reported that 51% of all supervisees reported at least one perceived ethical violation by their supervisors. The most frequently violated ethical principles related to guidelines regarding performance appraisal. This was followed in frequency by complaints regarding monitoring of supervisee's activities, confidentiality violations, sexual/dual relationships, blurring the line between psychotherapy and supervision, and termination/follow-up issues.

What was even of more significance in their study was the fact that, while over half of the supervisees felt they observed unethical behavior on the part of their supervisor, only 35% actually discussed these perceived violations with their supervisor. This does not mean, however, that they weren't talking about what they viewed as unethical behavior. Eighty-four percent discussed the potential violations with a peer or friend in the field, 33% discussed them with a significant other, and 14% of the time, someone in a position of power was informed about the situation, but took no action. As a supervisor, the core essence of your role is to model ethical behavior for your supervisees. If supervisors cut corners when it comes to ethical, professional behavior, it gives supervisees a license to do the same. When supervisees start pushing the limits of ethics, it often becomes a slippery slope leading to major ethical and professional violations.

Major Ethical Issues Related to Supervision

For a professional, supervising individuals inserts another dimension of complexity in attempting to function in an ethical fashion. Supervising other professionals adds to the number of cases that you ultimately have the responsibility for the provision of high quality services and ensuring that clients are not harmed. Instead of carrying a caseload of 50, supervisors legally carry responsibility for six or seven caseloads of 50.

Functioning ethically becomes more complicated. The major ethical concerns for a supervisor involves issues of competence, due process, informed consent, confidentiality, and multiple or dual relationships.

Major Ethical Issues Related to Supervision

Competence

Due Process

Informed Consent

Multiple/Dual Relationships

Competence

Unfortunately, for many, the practice of supervision is grounded in an assumption that a) a trained therapist will automatically be a good supervisor and b) having been supervised qualifies one to supervise. These assumptions are fallacious, as there is no guarantee that anyone is going to be a competent supervisor simply because they are a veteran or experienced clinician. The skill set required for supervision is substantially different from the skill set required for providing case services. While some individuals may possess both skill sets, other individuals may have great clinical experience but lack the necessary skills to be a supervisor.

The definition of competency to supervise varies from discipline to discipline, but most have three common components 1) formal education, 2) professional training, and 3) carefully supervised experience. The legal standard of competent practice within a discipline is often established by matching the skills, experience, and performance of an average fellow professional in good standing under similar circumstances. To the same extent, the standard of competence for supervision may imply that a supervisor closely matches the performance, skills, and abilities of a fellow professional supervisor in good standing.

To whatever extent my formal education, professional training, and supervised experience vary significantly from a fellow supervisor, it may raise issues of my competence as a supervisor. In some situations, individuals are hired to provide supervision, based on their education, for services that they have had little applicable or practical experience. An argument could be made that these individuals are acting outside their competence, violating the standard of care for supervision and violating specific principles of their profession's ethics code.

Professional groups such as, AAMFT, NBCC, and AAPC have specific criteria that must be attained to be an approved supervisor. NASW (2004) guidelines spell out 13 specific qualifications that must be attained by someone providing supervision, including: three years post masters experience, not currently under sanctions of any kind, demonstrating ongoing professional development, clinical expertise, and understanding of issues related to diversity.

A number of ethics codes specifically address the issue of competence in supervision. These ethics codes highlight the fact that an individual should only supervise within the scope of their competence; they should solely supervise activities that they themselves are competent to perform; and they only assign activities to supervisees, which they know the supervisee has the competence to perform.

> ➤ "Psychologists provide services, teach and conduct research....within the boundaries of their competence based on their education, training, supervised experience, consultation, study, or professional experience." APA (2002), 2.01
> ➤ "Counselors practice only within the boundaries of their competence, based on their education, training, supervised experience, state and national professional credentials, and appropriate professional experience.... Counselors accept employment only for positions which they are qualified by education, training, supervised experience, state and national professional credentials, and appropriate professional experience." ACA (2005), C.2.a and C.2.c's
> ➤ "Social workers who provide supervision or consultation should have the necessary knowledge and skill to supervise or consult appropriately and should do so only within their areas of knowledge and competence." NASW (2008) 3.01
> ➤ "Psychologists who delegate work to supervisees take reasonable steps to ....(2) authorize only those responsibilities that such persons can be expected to perform competently on the basis of their education, training, or experience, either independently or with the level of supervision being provided and (3) see that such persons perform these services competently." APA (2002), 2.05
> ➤ "Supervisors should teach courses and supervise clinical work only in areas where they are fully competent and experienced." ACES (1995) 3.02

Supervisory competence, viewed across a number of professions, has at least four elements: 1) having been trained in supervision and having appropriate supervisory experience, 2) acquiring an appropriate level of academic and professional credentials in the area which they are supervising, 3) demonstrating clinical experience in the area being supervised, and 4) competence in dealing with multicultural issues. Without these credentials, skills, abilities, and experiences it is very unlikely that you can be an effective and competent supervisor.

Pope and Vazquez (1998) distinguished between *intellectual competence*, i.e., education, knowledge, critical thinking, and conceptualization versus *emotional competence*, i.e., knowledge of self, self-monitoring, areas relevant to self-care. In their article, they assert that simply because a supervisor has the intellectual competence to supervise, i.e. appropriate degrees and experience, doesn't guarantee being a competent supervisor.

A competent supervisor has emotional competence in addition to intellectual requirements of supervision. A supervisor may have the right degrees, past experience, training in supervision, and ability to develop strategies, but may not be able to communicate these skills to a supervisee. The inability to interact effectively or connect on an interpersonal level with supervisees may seriously limit the effectiveness of a supervisor.

Pope and Vasquez (1998) pointed out that, in addition to developing our intellectual competence, supervisors also need to be working on developing emotional competence. This can be achieved by focusing on things like knowledge of self, awareness of your own stimulus value, your impact on other people, and the supervisor's level of burnout or compassion fatigue. A supervisor who is a "burnout" and is just going through the motions of supervision may be incompetent to supervise.

Due Process

An area for potential ethical issues in supervision would involve those supervisors who, as a result of the power differential, take advantage and exploit supervisees. Supervisees need to be informed of their rights and the appeal process available if they are in disagreement with an aspect of supervision or feel they are being treated unfairly. Supervisees need to know in advance what might constitute disciplinary action or termination and the proper notice that is required on the part of the supervisor. A competent supervisor communicates the opportunity for a formal hearing, defense, and/or appeal to their supervisor. Generally, supervisees have a right to a clear understanding of the requirements and expectations of supervision.

Since evaluation is a critically important aspect of supervision, supervisees need to know, and may have a legal right to know, in advance about evaluation criteria and the tools by which they will be evaluated. Supervisors may wish to consider providing their supervisees with a copy of the evaluation form and information about the evaluation process at the very first supervisory meeting. Due process rights may require supervisors to delineate and define what signals successful completion of the supervisory requirement. However, when possible, successful completion of the supervisory experience should be delineated in concrete terms such as the number of direct client contact hours, length of time, completion of reports, etc.

A number of professional ethics codes provide guidance and direction as to the requirement to insure a supervisee's due process rights.

> ➤ "Supervisors inform supervisees of the policies and procedures which they are to adhere and the mechanisms for due process appeal of individual supervisory actions." ACA (2005) F.4.a

> ➤ "Supervisors should incorporate the principles of informed consent and participation; clarity of requirements, expectations, roles and rules; and due process and appeal into the establishment of policies pursued and individual supervisory relationships. Mechanisms for due process appeal of individual supervisory actions should be established and made available to all supervisees." ACES (1995) 2.14

> ➤ "Social workers who provide supervision should evaluate a supervisee's performance in a manner that is fair and respectful...... Social workers who function as educators or field instructors for students should evaluate student's performance in a manner that is fair and respectful..... Social workers should accept employment or arrange to field placements only in organizations that exercise fair personal practices." NASW (2008) 3.0 1d; 3.02 b; and 3.09 f

Informed Consent

Informed consent is a concept that has been largely developed in the context of providing medical, psychological, and therapeutic services. As a general concept, informed consent allows for 1) elucidating expectations, 2) identifying mutually agreed upon goals, 3) anticipating likely difficulties, and 4) identifying the problem solving processes in advance (Guest & Dooley, 1999).

The concept of informed consent has recently been applied to supervisor/supervisee relationships and requires providing potential supervisees with information about the supervision that might reasonably influence their ability to make sound decisions about participation in supervision (Thomas, 2010). This concept has surfaced specifically in a number of professional ethical codes and standards, as well as in the professional literature.

❖ "When a psychologist conducts research or provide assessment, therapy, counseling, or consulting services in person or via electronic transmission or other forms of communication, they obtain informed consent of the individual or individuals." APA (2002) 3.10

❖ "In academic and supervisory relationships, psychologists establish a timely and specific process for providing feedback to students and supervisees. Information regarding the process is provided the student or supervisee at the beginning of supervision." APA (2002) 7.06

❖ "Supervisors are responsible for incorporating tutor supervision the principles of informed consent and participation. Supervisors inform supervisees of the policies and procedures to which they are to adhere in the mechanisms for due process appeal of individual supervisory actions." ACA (2005) F.4.a.

❖ "Supervisors should incorporate the principles of informed consent and participation; clarity of requirements, expectations, roles, and rules, and due process and appeal into the establishment of policies and procedures for their institution, program, courses, and individual supervisory relationships." ACES (1995) 2.14

> ❖ A written understanding should be signed by both the supervisor and supervisee (and the agency administrator) at the beginning of supervision and amended or renegotiated to reflect changes." NASW (1994) p.6

Bernard and Goodyear (2009) and Falvey (2002) suggest that informed consent takes place on multiple levels:

> ➢ Client's consent to treatment by a supervisee under a supervisor's direction
> ➢ Supervisor and supervisee consent to the supervisory responsibility
> ➢ The institution or agency consents to comply with clinical, legal, and ethical requirements
> ➢ The client consents to supervision of their case by a named individual
> ➢ Client's consent that confidential information will be shared with the supervisor.

Clients give informed consent to treatment, and a part of that informed consent is the awareness that the person they're receiving services from operates under supervision. In order for clients to provide informed consent to treatment, they may need know the specific identity of the supervisor to avoid dual relationships or conflicts of interest. Clients need to have a named supervisor in order to consent fully to information being shared. A simple statement that their case is being supervised may not be sufficient for true informed consent.

Finally, clients consent to the fact that confidential information will be shared. We assure clients of confidentiality and then immediately break that confidentiality by sharing information with supervisors. Even though we may be careful about discussing cases in terms of a client ID number or by first name, in some situations it can become readily apparent who you're talking about, particularly in rural communities or high-profile cases.

Informed consent for supervision has a number of key elements that must be discussed and disclosed. Thomas (2010) has identified a number of essential elements of informed consent for supervision.

Possible Elements to be included in an Informed Consent Document for Supervision, (Thomas, 2010)

1. Supervisory Methods
2. Confidentiality
3. Financial Issues
4. Documentation
5. Risks and Benefits
6. Evaluation Criteria/Procedures
7. Complaint Procedures
8. Termination Criteria
9. Supervisor's Responsibilities
10. Supervision Sessions Content
11. Supervisory Accessibility
12. Supervisee Responsibility
13. Informing the Supervisor
14. Professional Development Goals

Informed consent for supervision should provide a clear understanding of the purpose of supervision and what should be expected, including probable outcomes, risks, and benefits. Informed consent for supervision may require providing some information about the supervisor's credentials, clinical training, background, and theoretical perspective so that the supervisee can determine the "goodness of fit" between themselves and the prospective supervisor. Many particularly difficult situations could be avoided if both the potential supervisor and potential supervisee have a clear understanding in advance that they are coming from two completely different theoretical perspectives. Informed consent for supervision may need to involve a thorough discussion of the logistical aspects of supervision such as fees, documentation, the time and place of supervision, makeup sessions for supervision, emergency procedures, and evaluation. This informed consent can proactively eliminate potentially resolvable problems, or at least clarify the expectations of supervision. Informed consent for supervision needs to discuss issues of confidentiality, due process rights, legal and ethical issues, termination criteria and mutual responsibilities.

The following is an example of an Informed Consent for Supervision document that can be tailored to meet a particular supervision situation. Other fine examples of Informed Consent Agreements are available in Bernard & Goodyear (2009), Campbell (2006), Fallendar & Shafranske (2004), Falvey (2001), and Thomas (2010).

Informed Consent for Supervision

Purpose

The purpose of this form is to provide you with essential information about supervision and to ensure a common understanding about the supervision process.

Professional Disclosure

I earned my Doctorate in Clinical Psychology from Spalding University and am licensed as a Clinical Psychologist by the Commonwealth of Kentucky. I earned my undergraduate degree at Bellarmine University and my Master's Degree at Xavier University. I have received additional supervised training as a Marriage and Family Therapist and am licensed as a Marriage and Family Therapist by the Commonwealth of Kentucky. I am a member of the American Psychological Association, the Kentucky Psychological Association, and The American Association of Marriage and Family Therapists. My theoretical orientation combines a Behaviorist and Cognitive approach that is augmented by Systemic thinking and intervention. I have had extensive training and experience working with and evaluating children. My training and experience has not included extensive work in substance abuse, EMDR, or neuropsychological evaluations. These approaches should be considered out of my range of competence and will not be supervised by me. I have been a clinical supervisor for over 15 years and am current on the requirements for providing supervision as established by the Kentucky Board of Psychology.

Practical Issues

In order to fulfill the requirements for supervision, we will meet on Tuesdays at 10:00 a.m. in my office on the second floor of Theilard Hall. Weekly supervision will involve case review and videotape review of sessions, The supervisee is responsible for having a new tape available for review each week after the first two weeks of the practicum. If a holiday or vacation falls on Tuesday, we will reschedule for another day during that week. If a circumstance arises that makes it impossible for you to attend, it is your responsibility to notify me as soon as possible to make up the supervision. In addition to the one hour of face-to-face supervision, you are required to attend the trainee group supervision with Dr. Hall.

I will provide you with both formal and informal evaluation and feedback throughout your training during the course of supervisory meetings. I will also solicit information from Dr. Hall about your performance in the trainee group and will incorporate that as a part of the ongoing evaluation process. A formal summative evaluation will be completed at the end of each academic semester utilizing the format prescribed by the University. Evaluation will be based on the responsibilities, goals, and objectives established in the supervisory contract.

During the course of supervision, there may be disagreements about the strategies, interventions, procedures, processes, or other issues. The supervisee should surface these issues with the supervisor and an attempt will be made to resolve any conflict or disagreement. In the event that a satisfactory resolution cannot be achieved, the supervisee has the right to request a meeting with the Department Director, Dr. Barbara Smith, to attempt to resolve and mediate the dispute.

Legal and Ethical Issues

It is important that you agree to act in an ethical manner as outlined in the APA Code of Ethics, do not engage in dual relationships with clients, follow laws and regulations related to confidentiality, reporting abuse, and Duty to Warn. The supervisee agrees to always act in a fashion that will not jeopardize, harm, or be injurious or potentially damaging to clients. The supervisor will follow ethical codes and standards as it relates to treating supervisees with respect and dignity. Supervision is not intended to provide you with counseling or therapy, although personal issues may be surfaced and discussed as they relate to client treatment.

If personal issues or psychological/emotional concerns arise that interfere with or negatively impact client care, the supervisee agrees to seek outside counseling or other means to immediately resolve these issues. The content of our sessions will be considered confidential, except for the following: 1) the completion of the summative evaluation; 2) any situation where the treatment of a client violates legal or ethical standards; 3) any situation when problems or disagreements between us do not seem resolvable and outside consultation is required; and 4) situations where disciplinary action or termination of the supervisee is being considered.

Statement of Agreement

I have read and understand the information contained in this document, I have been provided a copy of the document, and agree to participate in supervision according to these guidelines.

Supervisee Signature   Date

Supervisor Signature   Date

The example covers a number of issues that are essential for a supervisee to be able to give informed consent for entering into a supervisory relationship. The first is a statement of purpose of supervision, which might vary from situation to situation. The purpose of supervision for students is different from supervision for licensure, and is also substantially different from supervision of a long-term staff member. Clarifying the purpose and nature of the supervisory relationship can avoid problem situations or misunderstandings from occurring. In order to give informed consent to entering into a supervisory relationship, supervisees need to have a basic awareness of the supervisor's professional background and credentials. Potential supervisees should know the supervisor's areas of competence and, more importantly, areas that the supervisor does not possess the competence for supervising.

Informed Consent allows the supervisor to address the practical, nitty-gritty issues of supervision in writing and can prevent future problems and misunderstandings. Identifying how evaluation will occur and who will be involved in that process is also a central component of giving informed consent and entering into a relationship with a well recognized power differential. Any special requirements for supervision that will occur can be spelled out in advance for supervisees in an informed consent agreement. Identifying due process rights and how that process can be accessed in the event of a problematic supervisory relationship is a key to informed consent. Spelling out due process rights in an informed consent prevents a supervisee from the defense of "no one told me about that" or "I didn't know I could appeal a supervisor's decision."

Legal and ethical issues are an area of emphasis for informed consent. Spelling out that supervisees are expected to adhere to a specific code of ethics, avoid dual relationships with clients, follow applicable laws, report abuse, and follow the Duty to Warn procedures protects the supervisor and supervisee. Addressing the question of personal issues interfering with service provision and spelling out that supervision is not to be considered therapy are part of giving informed consent.

Finally, addressing the issue of confidentiality in supervision and the limits of confidentiality in a supervisory relationship can prevent disastrous situations from occurring. Supervisees may mistakenly view supervision as synonymous with therapy and disclose information that can have serious implications.

Multiple/Dual Relationships

A major ethical concern in the supervisory relationships is multiple/dual relationships. Pope and Vasquez (1998) surveyed state Psychology Boards and found that sexual or dual relationships were the primary reasons for board complaints and disciplinary actions. Historically it has also been a major area of ethical concern for professional organizations. APA Ethics Committee (2008) reported that over 60% of all ethics cases opened included multiple relationships as one factor. Almost all professional ethical codes address the topic of dual relationships in supervisory situations.

> ➤ " A psychologist refrains from entering into a multiple relationship if the multiple relationship could reasonably be expected to impair the psychologist's objectivity, competence, or effectiveness in performing his or her functions as a psychologist, or otherwise risk exploitation or harm to the person with whom a professional relationship exists....Multiple relationships that would not reasonably be expected to cause impairment or risk of exploitation or harm are not unethical." APA (2002) 3.05.a
>
> ➤ "Psychologists do not exploit persons over whom they have supervisory, evaluative, or other authority, such as clients/patients, students, supervisees, research participants, and employees." APA (2002) 3.08

➤ "Supervisors who have multiple roles with supervisees should minimize potential conflicts. Where possible, the roles should be divided among several supervisors. Where this is not possible, careful explanation should be conveyed to the supervisee as to the expectations and responsibilities associated with each supervisory role." ACES (1995) 2.09

➤ "Counseling supervisors avoid nonprofessional relationships with current supervisees.....they do not engage in any form of nonprofessional interaction that may compromise the supervisory relationship." ACA (2005) F.3.a.

➤ "Members must not accept as supervisees those individuals with whom a prior or existing relationship could compromise the supervisor's objectivity.....examples of such relationships include, but are not limited to, those individuals with whom the therapist has a current or prior sexual, close personal, immediate familial, or therapeutic relationship. " AAMFT (2001) 4.3 and 4.6

➤ "A multiple relationship is one in which a psychologist is in a professional role, while simultaneously engaging in another role with that individual or someone closely associated with or related." APA (2002) 3.05.a

➤ "Supervisors should not engage in any form of social contact or interaction which would compromise the supervisor-supervisee relationship. Dual relationships with supervisees that might impair the supervisor's objectivity and professional judgment should be avoided and/or the supervisory relationship terminated " ACES (1995) 2.10

> ➤ "Social workers who function as educators or field instructors for students should not engage in any dual or multiple relationships with students in which there is a risk of exploitation or potential harm to the student." NASW (2008) 2.07

Multiple/dual relationships are a particularly difficult and problematic issue within the helping professions. "A multiple/dual relationship exists when a therapist or supervisor has a concurrent or consecutive personal, social, business, or professional relationship with a client or supervisee in addition to the therapist-client or supervisor–supervisee relationship, and these roles conflict or compete" (Kitchner, 1988). Supervisors have the responsibility for closely scrutinizing and monitoring the relationship that exists between themselves and their supervisees to prevent harm or exploitation. The question that must be asked repeatedly during a supervisory relationship is to what extent, if any, is my judgment as a supervisor impaired by a multiple or dual relationship. Duality cannot be avoided completely, but it can be managed thoughtfully and judiciously.

A discrimination that is critical in making an ethical assessment of the situation is determining how discrepant a secondary relationship is from the primary role as the supervisor. The greater the divergence between the nature of the relationships, the greater the risk of harm. To this end, some ethics codes specifically prohibit supervising family members (AAMFT, 2007). Campbell (2006) notes, "application of these principles to small communities, rural settings, religious groups, gay, feminist, and ethnic minorities may be more complex and problematic." AAPC (1997) acknowledges (and therefore, allows) that supervision may occur between individuals who have social and collegial relationships, "but supervisors are directed to structure the interactions so as not to interfere with the successful fulfillment of the supervisory contract."

A fundamental distinction, which must be made in managing and regulating supervisory multiple/dual relationships, is the distinction between a *boundary crossing* and a *boundary violation.* "A boundary is the defined 'edge' of appropriate or professional behavior, transgression of which involves the therapist stepping out of the clinical role." ..... "a 'slippery slope' refers to seemingly insignificant erosions in boundaries that may transform into significant violations....The erosion or benign boundary crossings may be either a precipitant or a predictor of a sexual relationship that ensues" (Lamb and Catanzaro, 1998).

A *boundary crossing* is a non-pejorative term that describes departures from commonly accepted clinical practice that may or may not benefit the supervisee. Boundary crossings may be harmless, non-exploitative, or even supportive. Boundary crossings should be viewed as potentially high-risk behaviors and may include issues of money, place and space, gifts, services, clothing, language, self-disclosure, and physical contact. A *boundary violation* is a clear departure from acceptable practice that places the supervisee or the supervisory process at serious risk (Lamb and Catanzaro, 1998).

Guthell & Gabbard (1993) identified what they considered to be The Seven Deadly Boundary Crossings. The areas of potential boundary crossings that they identified included: time, place, money, gifts/favors, clothing, language, and physical contact. Your normal practice of supervision, and what is generally accepted as standard practice for supervision, involves certain typical elements such as time and place, dress, language, and physical contact. Any variation from the common practice of supervision is a boundary crossing that has the potential to lead to boundary violations.

Changing the location of supervision to take place outside of the office or rescheduling supervision at a time beyond normal business hours, in and of themselves, may not be problematic. However, these are clearly examples of boundary crossings that have the potential to lead to more serious boundary violations, and therefore should be meticulously considered. Introducing the element of money, gifts, or favors into the supervisory relationship has the potential to change the relationship and these are areas that must be dealt with cautiously or completely avoided in supervision.

Ethical human service professionals typically have a very clear understanding of boundaries with clients or patients and religiously guard and defend those boundaries. Few professionals would consider engaging in recreational activities with clients, attending a party at a client's house, going to lunch with a client, or going out after work with a client. On the other hand, playing on the agency's softball team with a supervisee, attending an agency party where a supervisee is present, going to lunch with a supervisee or group of supervisees, or even going out after work with supervisees, in and of themselves, are not necessarily ethical boundary violations. However, they are certainly boundary crossings that could lead to more fundamental problems.

The difficulty with multiple or dual relationships with supervisees is that supervisees are also coworkers, colleagues, and fellow professionals. This may naturally create the opportunity for dual relationships. Some supervisors adopt an absolute stance in this regard and do not engage with the supervisees in any fashion other than in regular ongoing supervision. Other supervisors may still be principled who take a more relaxed attitude about certain activities that they do not feel would impact their ability to provide ethical supervision or an objective evaluation.

Dual relationships that affect our ability to practice professionally and ethically can be very difficult to avoid entirely. As discussed earlier, in the situation of the supervisor who has both administrative as well as clinical supervisory responsibilities, that, in and of itself, constitutes a dual relationship. It may not be unethical, but is clearly a dual relationship. The application of these principles can become particularly difficult if you work in a small community, or rural setting, where everybody knows everybody, and there are inevitably a variety of interconnections.

For individuals who are pastoral counselors, totally avoiding dual relationships in small religious groups where there are limited pastoral counselors doing supervision may be

103

problematic. Doing supervision with a church member means that I may also have to deal with that person at church, or we may be sitting on the same committee discussing church business. Dual relationships should be avoided whenever possible, but in many situations it may not be totally possible to avoid all dual relationships with supervisees. A dual relationship that can and must be avoided with supervisees is a violation of sexual boundaries.

Supervisor – Supervisee Sexual Relationships

The simple answer is – what part of "no" don't you understand. It is very difficult to imagine any set of circumstances where being involved with a supervisee in a romantic or sexual relationship could be justified. Ethics codes have specific prohibitions regarding sexual contact with supervisees and students (AAPC, ACA, APA, ASPPB, CPA, AAMFT, and NASW) and do not allow for exceptions. The American Psychiatric Association (2009) is the one professional organization allowing for exceptions and states that "sexual contact between a supervisor and a trainee or student **may** be unethical."

"Sexual or romantic interactions or relationships with current supervisees are prohibited..... Counseling Supervisors avoid accepting close relatives, romantic partners, or friends of supervisees." ACA (2005) F.3 b/c.

"Supervisors do not participate in any form of sexual contact with supervisees." ACES (1995)

"Social workers who function as supervisors or educators should not engage in sexual activities or contact with supervisees, students, trainees, or other colleagues over whom they exercise professional authority........ Social workers should not sexually harass supervisees, students, trainees, or colleagues. Sexual harassment includes sexual advances, sexual solicitation, requests for sexual favors, and other verbal or physical conduct of a sexual nature." NASW (2008) 2.07

"Marriage and family therapist do not engage in sexual intimacy with students or supervisees during the evaluative or training relationship between the therapist and the student or supervisor. Should a supervisor engage in sexual activity with a former supervisee, the burden of proof shifts to the supervisor to demonstrate that there has been no exploitation or injury to the supervisee." AAMFT (2001) 4.3

"Psychologists do not engage in sexual relationships with students or supervisees who are in their department, agency, or training center or over whom psychologists have or are likely to have evaluative authority." APA (2002) 7.07

Many supervisors and supervisees would prefer to minimize the issue of sexual intimacy between supervisors and supervisees, almost to the point of denial. The seminal study on the issue was conducted by Glaser and Thorpe (1986) in which they surveyed female members of APA Division 12, Clinical Psychology. Their survey indicated that 17% of respondents reported having had sexual contact with psychology educators/supervisors as graduate students. In addition, 31% reported having experienced seductive behavior with educators/supervisors while they were in professional training.

A replication of the study by Hammel, Olkin, and Taube (1996) reported that rates of supervisor-supervisee sexual relationships had dropped to 10% and this rate was sustained in a more recent study (Lamb and Catanzaro, 2003). A variety of studies have since reported rates of supervisor-supervisee sexual relationships to be consistently between 1.5 to 4 %. Lamb and Catanzaro (1998) place the rate of supervisor – supervisee sexual contact between 3% and 8%. A more recent study by Zakrewski (2006) reported rates of 2%, but the sample included male and female students. In that study, women were 2.5 times more likely to have had sexual contact with a supervisor than men.

The impact of a sexual or dual relationship on the supervisory process should not be underestimated. As a consequence of the dual relationship, the supervisee is no longer as comfortable confronting or disagreeing with the supervisor. The supervisor's ability to evaluate the supervisee objectively is severely compromised by the nature of the dual relationship. A dual or sexual relationship places the supervisor in legal jeopardy to accusations of inadequate supervision or the accusation of unfairness in evaluation. Supervisees involved in a dual relationship with their supervisor run the risk of isolation from the work group by peers, perceived preferential treatment, and questioning of professional judgment (Zakrewski, 2006). Supervisors may consciously or unconsciously over accommodate or show favoritism to a supervisee with whom they have a dual relationship.

Some authors would make an argument that a sexual relationship between two consenting adults, who happen to be supervisor and supervisee, is not necessarily problematic (Lazarus and Zur, 2002). Celenza (2007) and other authors make very strong arguments, to the contrary. "Because of the power differential and the supervisee's vulnerability implicit in supervisee/supervisor sexual relationships, *completely voluntary consent may be impossible* in supervisee/supervisor sexual relationships. Thus, to argue that such a relationship is consensual may be fallacious." (Koocher & Keith-Spiegel, 1998). "The power differential in a supervisory dyad can create unique vulnerabilities for supervisees" (Gottlieb, Robinson, & Younggren, 2007).

In many situations, what started out as "consensual" often takes on a different feeling when the relationship ends or goes sour. Glaser and Thorpe (1986) reported that 28% of those involved in a sexual relationship with the supervisor felt some coercion at the time, but in retrospect 51% reported feeling that they were coerced into a relationship. More tragically, supervisees who were sexually involved with supervisors are more likely to become offenders themselves (Bartell and Rubin, 1990 and Pope et al., 1979).

Socialization with Supervisees

While sexual boundaries are probably the most egregious form of a dual relationship, it certainly is not the only area where a dual relationship can occur. Navin et al. (1995) reported that 25 percent of field based supervisors were aware of social interactions between supervisors and supervisees that may be incompatible with a supervisor's duties. The collegial nature of supervision may cause supervisors to lose sight of their evaluation responsibilities and their need to be in a position of objectivity. Social interaction between supervisors and supervisees may appear to be benign, or even beneficial, yet social interactions with supervisees pose some ethical risks. The core ethical question is: How does the socialization enhance or inhibit the professional relationship? *"Social contact that compromises the supervisory relationship or that might impair the supervisor's objectivity and professional judgment should be avoided."* (ACES, 1993).

What may have appeared to be appropriate social interactions with supervisees, such as attending a party or participating on the agency softball team, can become acutely problematic when something goes very, very wrong. There can also be a potential problem with a perception of favoritism toward a supervisee due to socialization. Some supervisors adopt a policy of not socializing in any form with supervisees for as long as the person is an active supervision. Others may take a more flexible approach and judge situations on a case-by-case basis. Haynes et al (2003) provides some guidance in this area by setting forth questions that supervisors should pose to themselves for consideration while making decisions about socialization.

Could the socializing impact my ability to give a negative evaluation or terminate a supervisee?

> Can I explain and justify my decisions around socializing to an ethics board?
> What advice would I give a colleague in a similar situation?
> In my setting, how appropriate is socializing and what is the professional maturity of my supervisee?
> How might other supervisees react knowing that I am socializing with some supervisees, but not all of them?
> How comfortable am I with my actions being known publicly or by my boss?
> What is the worst possible scenario that could emerge from my decision to socialize with a supervisee?

Summary

In summary, supervision is an area of practice that is rife with ethical concerns and considerations. All professional ethical codes devote considerable discussion to the topic and address a number of specific issues about the supervisor-supervisee relationship. In order to be an ethical supervisor, supervisors must be competent and well trained, knowledgeable of ethics codes, create a structure for supervision, have clearly defined evaluation criteria and dialogue about dual relationships and multicultural issues. Ethical supervisors utilize Informed Consent, establish goals and objectives for supervision, document supervision activities, and regularly consult with other supervisors about their supervision.

The fifth most frequent reason for an ethical complaint being filed with licensing boards was improper or inadequate supervision. While most supervisors view themselves as supervising in an ethical fashion, a supervisee's perceptions of the ethics of their supervisor are very different. While most supervisors are reluctant to confront their supervisor's questionable ethics, most likely due to the power differential, many will discuss it with colleagues and friends.

Major ethical issues involving supervision typically involve issues of competence, due process, informed consent, and multiple and dual relationships. Supervisors must limit their supervisory activities to areas where they can demonstrate formal education, professional training, and supervised experience. Ethics codes and professional organizations have attempted to address standards for competence to supervise through criteria and ongoing training. Supervisory competence, viewed across a number of professions, has at least four elements: 1) having been trained in supervision and having appropriate supervisory experience, 2) acquiring an appropriate level of academic and professional credentials in the area which they are supervising, 3) demonstrating clinical experience in the area being supervised, and 4) competence in dealing with multicultural issues. A supervisor must also possess emotional stability and maturity to competently supervise.

The concept of informed consent has recently been applied to supervisor/supervise relationships and requires providing potential supervisees with information about the supervision that might reasonably influence their ability to make sound decisions about participation in supervision. Many particularly difficult situations could be avoided if both the potential supervisor and potential supervisee have a clear understanding in advance of supervision demands and expectations.

Multiple/dual relations are a particularly problematic area in supervision. Duality cannot be completely avoided, but must be managed in an ethical and thoughtful fashion. Boundary crossings between a supervisor and supervisee, while in and of themselves, are not unethical can ultimately lead to boundary violations and unethical practices. Sexual relationships are the most obvious crossing of boundaries between a supervisor and supervisee, but there are other areas such as time, place, money, gifts/favors, clothing, language, and physical contact. Almost all ethical codes for the helping professions specifically prohibit sexual contact between supervisors and supervisees. While the incidence of sexual relationships between supervisors and supervisees has declined, recent studies would indicate that the rate has stabilized at approximately 3 to 8 percent. The impact of a sexual relationship between a supervisor and supervisee can have a markedly negative impact on the supervisory relationship, and by extension on client services. Some authors would question whether a completely consensual sexual relationship between a supervisor and supervisee is even possible given the power differential and the professional implications.

While sexual relationships between a supervisor and supervisee are obviously problematic and unethical, a more subtle but problematic supervisory ethical conundrum relates to socializing between supervisors and supervisees. Social contact that compromises the supervisory relationship or that might impair the supervisor's objectivity and professional judgment should be avoided, but may be impossible to avoid completely.

CHAPTER FIVE

Legal Issues in Clinical Supervision

DISCLAIMER - Legal issues related to supervision vary significantly from jurisdiction to jurisdiction and from profession to profession. In dealing with specific questions regarding legal issues in supervision, it may be necessary to consult with an attorney licensed in your particular jurisdiction. The following discussion attempts to provide basic information regarding the nature of legal issues that are frequently observed across jurisdictions and across professions. These may serve as a general guide and provide a conceptual understanding of these issues; however, specific situations may require more in-depth analysis by a legal professional.

Many seminars I have attended about legal and ethical issues of supervision seemed to have the focus of attempting to scare people about the legal and ethical issues of supervision. It is true that you have assumed additional legal and ethical risks once you take on the task of supervision, but this should not create an atmosphere of fear. It is not my intent to scare supervisors or potential supervisors, but to provide sufficient information to make suitable decisions that reflect an understanding of the legal and ethical issues associated with supervision. My hope is to inform you of the legal and ethical issues in such a way that you will attempt to "clean up some of the loose ends," and institute appropriate risk management strategies. Supervisors need to be realistic about the reality of the fact that the moment they assumed supervisory responsibilities, they assumed greater risk of liability and potential ethical violations.

Part of that reality is the fact that as soon as you became a supervisor, you increased the risks that you may be sitting in a chair in the state office building answering questions put to you by a licensing board. By becoming a supervisor, you increased the risks that you may have to defend yourself and/or your supervisee's actions in a circuit court hearing. Due to the increased statistical risks, it is important that supervisors understand some basic legal principles and the impact those principles have on the practice of supervision.

Falvey (2001) outlines five general legal principles that must be understood in order to guide you to practice effective risk management.

> **Standard of Care** - The normative or expected practice performed in a given situation by a given group of professionals.
>
> **Statutory Liability** - Specific written standards with penalties imposed, written directly into the law.
>
> **Negligence** - When one fails to observe the proper standard of care.
>
> **Direct Liability** - Being responsible for your own actions or authority and control over others.
>
> **Vicarious Liability** - Being responsible for the actions of others based on being in a position of authority and control.

The **standard of care** is a rather loosely defined, constantly changing, and gradually emerging principle regarding the practice of a profession that the general public should be able to rely upon. A more concrete example may provide some focus and clarity. When seeking services from any professional licensed the public has a right to expect certain things and practices. In dentistry for example, current expectations are very different than the practice of dentistry in the 1860's, and have evolved over time. The standard of care has also changed as technology and materials have advanced over time. Individuals have a right to receive dental care consistent with current practices, current technology, and current knowledge regarding dentistry.

If you seek services from a licensed dentist, and three months later you find out that your dentist had this crazy idea that in order to preserve water and energy, she was only going to sterilize instruments every six months. That clearly violates the standard of care for dentistry. If you later develop a blood born disease, you will likely be able to hold the dentist liable as she certainly violated the standard of care for her profession. There is a standard of care for providing mental health or educational services to clients, and there is an emerging standard of care for supervision.

Statutory liability is the principle that there are certain requirements to practice your profession, which are spelled out in statutes or administrative regulations. If you choose to ignore or violate the requirements spelled out in the statutes, you will likely be found criminally or civilly liable. Almost all states have mandatory child abuse reporting laws. If you fail to report, or choose not to report child abuse, you could be held accountable and fined or even imprisoned.

Negligence, or when a professional fails to observe the standard of care, is an important legal concept that as a supervisor you must understand. You can be negligent as a supervisor by failing to observe, either intentionally or even unintentionally, the appropriate standard of care as it relates to the supervision. There are reasonable expectations about supervision, not the least of which is that supervision actually takes place. In a court setting or a board complaint, a supervisee may produce documentation that during the 52 weeks of supervision, the supervisor canceled supervision 26 times. This is a clear indication of failure on the supervisor's part to meet the duties and responsibilities of supervision, and is possible negligence. The failure to supervise consistently and in a timely fashion may have caused injury to a client, or at a minimum may not have provided adequate quality control or allowed for growth and development of the supervisee.

An important legal distinction involves two other legal concepts: **direct liability** and **vicarious liability**. In direct liability, if I do something, which results in damages to someone or something, I can be held directly liable. If I am driving while texting, putting on my make-up, and eating my breakfast, and I run into a car, I may have direct liability for the damages involved.

In addition, there is also the concept of vicarious liability, and this is particularly relevant as it relates to supervision. Vicarious liability is being legally responsible for the actions of others based on the fact that I, as the supervisor, was in a position of authority and control. My position of authority makes me accountable and liable for the actions of those that I am directing.

Standard of Care

The standard of care is a legal concept that has emerged from specific case law, ethics codes, professional standards, and the current status of the profession. The standard of care has emerged over time as a part of commonly accepted practice of a profession. At its core, the standard of care involves an element of competency. People seeking services from professionals, particularly licensed and regulated professionals, have the right to expect that when they seek services that the professional is competent to provide those services. If an individual is providing services without appropriate credentials or under falsified credentials, they are violating the standard of care, and you may have a claim against them if some damages occur.

Part of the standard of care may relate to confidentiality. Within certain limitations, individuals seeking service have an expectation of confidentiality. If a professional violates that confidentiality and damages occur, the individual may have a legitimate claim of liability and an expectation of compensation for damages. The standard of care also has implications for dual relationships. Seeking services from a professional doesn't mean that I am consenting to subject myself to a sales pitch about cleaning products or about the value of investing in vacation properties. Saccuzzo (1997) identified five major principles that were repeatedly found in statutes, case law, ethical codes, and professional literature related to the standard of care: 1) Competence, 2) Confidentiality, 3) Dual Relationships, 4) Welfare of Consumer, and 5) Informed Consent.

Fallendar and Shafranske (2004) stated that the Standards of Care for Supervision can be extracted from case law, ethics, statutes, and clinical practice. These included:

> ➢ Supervising only within your area of competence
> ➢ Providing appropriate feedback and evaluation
> ➢ Consistent monitoring and controlling of supervised activities
> ➢ Accurately documenting supervisory activities
> ➢ Providing consistent and timely supervision.

The Standard of Care for Supervision is an emerging and changing concept that has evolved over time. It is a composite of case law, statutes, administrative regulations, ethics codes, and the current professional literature. A major accepted part of the standard of care for supervision is that supervisors only supervise those activities that are within their area of competence. If I have no experience in treating eating disorders, and it just so happens that one of my supervisee is assigned a case involving an eating disordered client, the Standard of Care for Supervision may require reassigning the case, bringing in another supervisor as a consultant, or that another supervisor assume responsibility for supervising that case.

To allow a supervisee to provide services involving techniques or a diagnosis that the supervisor has no familiarity with is very likely a violation of the Standard of Care for Supervision. How can the supervisor be monitoring and controlling activities of which they have no familiarity or competence? Supervising outside my area of competence may involve ethical and legal liability.

Another reasonable expectation of the activity of supervision that could be considered as part of the standard of care is that the supervisor will provide the supervisee with feedback and evaluation. This is essential so that the supervisee can correct errors, improve skills, and develop to their maximum potential as a clinician. Many laissez-faire supervisors who approach supervision casually or with an attitude of "let's get this over with" may not make the effort to provide their supervisee with accurate and timely feedback so that adjustments in care can be provided. Some supervisors would rather spend the hour of supervision discussing the latest agency gossip, sports scores, or regaling the supervisee with "war stories" of their therapeutic exploits. While the stories and gossip may be interesting, they do little toward improving the quality of care that a specific client is receiving from their caseworker.

Part of the Standard of Care for Supervision is the expectation that supervisors consistently monitor and control case activity. As the supervisor, one of your functions is the monitoring of supervisee's work to ensure quality and protect clients. A basic familiarity with the supervisee's cases and an awareness of what the supervisee is doing or attempting to accomplish with those cases is essential. Failure to be knowledgeable about supervised case is an obvious impairment of the supervisory responsibility to monitor and control the supervisee's work activity.

Some of the activities that a supervisor might be engaged in order to be knowledgeable about cases and conscientiously monitoring and controlling a supervisee's activity would include: reviewing work samples, viewing videotapes, listening to audiotapes sitting in on cases with a supervisee, a joint home visit, reviewing treatment plans, and signing off on progress notes. Failure to engage in these, or similar, activities may make it very difficult to present a credible argument that you are effectively monitoring and controlling a supervisee's activity.

Another part of the Standard of Care for Supervision is documenting supervisory activities. Doing supervision without some form of written documentation is roughly the equivalent of providing services without keeping a case record. That would be both ethically and possibly legally disastrous. The old legal adage of "if it isn't in writing, it didn't happen" probably applies in the situation where you were providing adequate supervision, but there is no actual record of it occurring.

Some supervisors, particularly if you are dealing with a veteran staff, may have a more casual attitude about supervision and do not feel that documenting supervisory activity is necessary. This is like "working without a net" and operating under the assumption that nothing could possibly go wrong. Well, it can. Not keeping supervision documentation is a *prima facie case* of inadequate, unethical supervision and a clear departure from the Standard of Care for supervision. In situations where something does go wrong, what is likely to prevent liability from being assessed is that you can point to documentation of specific instructions to a supervisee or to a specific discussion with a supervisee. Being able to present supervisory notes that indicate your awareness of and attempts to provide appropriate feedback and monitoring the quality of services being delivered is clear evidence that you were attempting to practice within the Supervisory Standard of Care.

Finally, failure to provide supervisees with consistent and timely supervision is one of the most frequent reasons cited as a violation of the Standard of Care for Supervision. A large number of complaints about supervisors heard by licensing boards and professional associations are for failure to provide consistent and timely supervision. A variety of ethical codes specifically address the concept of providing consistent and timely supervision.

The supervisor who fails to show up for supervision, who cancels supervision regularly, who does not devote the required time for supervision, or who always has another higher priority meeting or client crisis, is not providing supervision on a consistent and timely basis. Allowing great periods of time to pass without meeting with a supervisee may put clients directly at risk because a supervisee was relying on having access to their supervisor to go over a complication in a case. Often when supervision was canceled or not held, supervisees were left to handle a potentially risky situation on their own.

Negligence/Malpractice

Malpractice is professional negligence and is therefore, a *tort*. A *tort* is a wrong that involves a breach of a civil duty owed to someone else. A person who suffers a tortuous injury is entitled to receive "damages", usually monetary compensation, from the person or people responsible — or liable — for those injuries. The most prominent tort liability is negligence. If the injured party can prove that the person believed to have caused the injury acted negligently - that is, without taking reasonable care to avoid injuring others - tort law will allow for compensation. A successful malpractice suit must demonstrate the "four D's" *Dereliction of a Duty Directly causing Damages.* (Bennie et al., 1998)

To establish that a supervisor has acted negligently, there are four legal criteria that must be established:

1. There was a **duty** to perform an action as established by the nature of the relationship or by statute.
2. There was a **breach** of the established duty, a violation of a standard of care that was foreseeable and unreasonable.
3. There is direct **causation** – breach of duty or care that was the direct, or proximate cause of the injury.
4. **Damages** occurred as a result of the action or lack of action of the supervisor, i.e., physical, financial, or emotional injury or damages.

Bennett et al. (1990) and Guest and Dooley (1999) expanded these concepts in the context of supervision:

➢ A professional relationship was formed between the supervisor and supervisee.
➢ There is a demonstrable standard of care for supervision, and the supervisor beached that standard.
➢ The supervisee or client suffered demonstrable harm or injury.
➢ The supervisor's breach of duty to practice within the standard of care was the *proximate cause* (reasonably foreseeable) of the supervisee's or client's injury.

When a supervisor enters into a supervisory relationship, that supervisee and indirectly all of their clients have a right to expect that the supervisor will engage in certain activities to monitor the quality of the service and direct the supervisee's activities. A breach in that relationship and obligation is where the supervisor does something to violate that standard of care, like not showing up for 50 percent of the supervision sessions. In that situation, the supervisor has probably breached their duty to perform and therefore may be negligent in that regard.

Another part of supervisory negligence that must be proven is to show causation. A major part of negligence is that there has to be demonstrable proof of causation of damages. If breaching the duty as a supervisor can be demonstrated to be the cause of damages taking place to a client or a supervisee, then negligence or malpractice may have occurred, and damages could be awarded.

Finally, as a part of negligence, there must be demonstrable damages. A supervisor is not negligent if they simply do something the supervisee does not like or disagrees with. A plaintiff or supervisee must be able to demonstrate that financial damages, physical damages, or emotional damages have occurred, and they have a right to be made whole. A supervisee might claim that a supervisor gave them a biased or unfair evaluation as a result of failing to execute properly their supervisory responsibilities. Pursuant to that evaluation, the supervisee might have been unable to be licensed, and therefore, they were unable to make a living or suffered a loss of income. A supervisor could possibly be found negligent, and be held liable for the loss of income that the supervisee suffered as a result of the supervisor's negligence.

Supervisory malpractice involves lawsuits filed by a supervisee or a client against a supervisor who has allegedly violated professional supervision practice standards. Failure to adequately supervise students or assistants is one of the ten most common causes of malpractice lawsuits (Stromberg and Dellinger, 1993). State Psychology Licensing Boards reported that inadequate or improper supervision ranked fifth in frequency among violations (Reaves, 1998). Harris (2003) identified supervisors as being at high risk of experiencing licensing board complaints due to the nature of the supervisory relationship.

Direct versus Vicarious Liability

As a supervisor, you have legal responsibility for the actions of your supervisees. "The supervisee is legally an agent of the supervising psychologist" (Knapp & Vandecreek, 2006). Legal liability (Johnson, 1995; Saccuzo, 2002) permeates all areas of supervisory responsibility, but most particularly, issues related to client welfare, professional development, and gate keeping.

For those individuals supervising, a key legal distinction that must be understood is the distinction between direct liability and vicarious liability. **Direct liability** is based on erroneous, improper, or unethical actions or omissions on the part of the supervisor. In the case of direct liability, if an individual takes some kind of action, or fails to act, and as a result another individual is damaged in some way, direct liability accrues. If a supervisor does something and causes damages to an individual, the supervisor may have liability and an obligation to make the person whole by paying damages.

Harrar, VandeCreek, and Knapp (1990) summarized direct liability as including: any action or lack of action that is a dereliction in carrying out the responsibility to adequately supervise a supervisee's work. This could include not supervising consistently or in a timely basis, not adequately monitoring a supervisee's caseload, failure to provide emergency coverage or crisis procedures, or not providing clear expectations or a supervisory contract. Giving a supervisee an inappropriate treatment recommendation that the supervisee implements to the client's detriment may result in direct liability on the part of the supervisor.

Other examples of situations where the supervisor might incur direct liability are: 1) assigning tasks to the supervisee which the supervisor knew, or should have known, the supervisee was inadequately trained to handle, 2) allowing a supervisee to practice outside his/her scope of practice, 3) failure to assess the supervisee's skills and abilities, and 4) failure to listen carefully to a supervisee's comments and therefore, failing to comprehend the client's needs. Lack of consistent feedback prior to the evaluation, a biased or unfair evaluation, or violating professional boundaries are obvious direct failings on the part of a supervisor for which they can be held directly liable.

In addition to having direct liability for my actions as a supervisor, the concept of **vicarious liability** means that the supervisor may also be liable for the actions of those individuals they supervise. Vicarious liability holds that supervisors are liable for their supervisee's actions because a) they are in a position of responsibility and authority, b) the supervisee was under the direct control of the supervisor, and c) the supervisor, or supervisor's agency or organization, may profit from the actions of their supervisees (Behnke et al., 1998). As a supervisor, even though I did nothing wrong, if my supervisee caused damages, the supervisor may hold some accountability for the actions of their supervisees. Saccuzzo (1997) stated that "supervisors can be liable not only for their own negligence in failing to supervise adequately, but also for the actions of their supervisee."

Vicarious Liability is based on the concepts of *respondeat superior, borrowed servant rule, or enterprise liability* (Falvey, 2001).

Respondeat Superior – liability attaches for a supervisee's actions because the supervisor has the authority and control, even if they lack specific knowledge about the situation. Liability attaches whether or not the supervisor personally breached a duty. "One who occupies a position of authority or direct control over another (such as a master and servant, employer and employee, or supervisor and supervisee) can be held legally liable for the damages another suffered as a result of the negligence of the subordinate" (Disney and Stephens, 1994). To whatever extent a supervisor has the ability and responsibility to control the activities of a supervisee, the supervisor has responsibility and liability for their supervisee's actions.

Borrowed Servant - liability attaches to the person who had control of the supervisee at the time of the negligent act. Liability may attach to the actions of my agents, representatives, or employees if they were acting on my behalf. This can become clouded when a supervisee is assigned or on loan from another entity, such as a student assigned to an agency for practicum or internships. Essential in determining supervisory liability is whether a person is subject to another's control with regard not only to the work to be conducted, but also the manner of performing that work (Sacuzzo, 1997).

Enterprise Liability – liability attaches to the extent that the supervisor or organization benefits or profits from the work of the supervisee. If a supervisor, or their organization, profits from the activities of a supervise, the liability for the supervisor's actions and activity increases. The possibility to gain from a supervisory relationship changes the nature of the relationship. The nature of the relationship creates additional liability and may create a dual relationship. The California Board of Psychology (2008) prohibits supervision for pay of prospective licensees. ASPPB (2003) spells out the differing nature of a supervisory relationship to the extent that "payment for supervision by a pre-doctoral supervisee is not acceptable."

Disney and Stephens (1994) clarified factors that aid in the determination of whether the supervisee's negligence implicated the supervisor, resulting in vicarious liability. These factors included, the supervisor's power to control the supervisee and the supervisee's duty to perform the act. Was the supervisee acting in a fashion consistent with their duties and obligations? Other factors that might mitigate vicarious liability for the supervisor included the time, place, and purpose of the act, the motivation of the supervisee for engaging in the act, and finally, whether the supervisor could have reasonably expected that the supervisee might commit the act. There are some behaviors that a supervisee might engage in that are inappropriate, but so far beyond the realm of a reasonable possibility, that it would not be rational for a supervisor to be monitoring and controlling for that activity.

Vicarious liability becomes a concern to supervisors as a result of their supervisee's inappropriate actions. There is a substantial body of case law that would indicate that supervisors can be liable not only for what they knew, but also if their negligence created a situation where they should have known a supervisee was acting inappropriately. *Simmons v. United States (1986)* held that supervisors assume direct responsibility for their response to supervisee sexual transgressions with clients. Supervisors have responsibility for overseeing the counseling relationship between the supervisee and client and *should know* what is taking place.

In *Simmons v. United States (1986)* a social worker who was being supervised initiated a sexual relationship with a client. A Tribal Chairwoman approached the supervisor and expressed concern about the relationship. The supervisor took no action to investigate the improper counseling relationship or remove the social worker from the case. The client ultimately attempted suicide when the relationship ended. The Court found that negligence is imposed on one who should have known of the negligent acts of a subordinate and the supervisor should have supervised the worker more closely so that he would have been aware of the situation at a much earlier date.

As a supervisor you may be legally vulnerable if you fail to take appropriate actions (*Andrews v. United States, 1984, cited in* Falendar and Shafranske, *2004*). A supervisor failed to investigate a report that an intern was having a sexual relationship with a client. By not speaking with the patient, conducting an investigation, or filing a written report, the supervisor was found liable, since he negligently failed to respond appropriately to a complaint of sexual misconduct.

Many individuals who currently supervise operate under a fairly naïve and false presumption that they are immune to any adverse legal problems due to their experience and professionalism. Pope and Tabachnick (1993) found that 11.6 % of respondents reported at least one malpractice lawsuit or board complaint. Miller (2002) stated that the possibility of an adverse disciplinary event during a 15 year career is 10 to 15%.

It is statistically unlikely that many supervisors will find themselves named in a lawsuit or criminal action. However, supervisors may find themselves more frequently facing a licensing board complaint. In many instances, it may actually be better to be facing a civil action than a licensing board complaint. The legal system offers built-in protections, such as rules of evidence and a standard of proof. If an individual is charged with a capital offense, they must be found guilty "beyond a reasonable doubt," or in more common parlance, at a level of about 95% certainty. If an individual is charged with a felony complaint the standard of proof in most legal systems is a "clear and convincing" or about 75% proof. In a civil action, the standard of proof is only a "preponderance of the evidence" or greater than 51%.

Many licensing boards have not established standards of proof and often utilize whatever criteria they feel are appropriate given the circumstances in order to protect the public from unscrupulous or incompetent practitioners. In a court, there are also specific requirements regarding hearsay testimony, third-party testimony, and admission of prior acts. These rules may or may not apply in a licensing board hearing.

Summary

Supervision is an activity that has major legal implications and risk as an inherent part of the activity. A number of legal principles have direct applicability to the process of supervision, including: standard of care, statutory liability, negligence, and direct and vicarious liability. The standard of care is loosely defined as the norm or expected practice performed in a given situation by a given group of professionals. The standard of care would require supervisors to only supervise within their area of competence and provide appropriate feedback and evaluations of a supervisee's activity. The standard of care for supervision would also include consistently monitoring and controlling a supervisee's activity, documenting supervisory activities, and providing consistent and timely supervision.

Malpractice is professional negligence. Supervisory malpractice or negligence implies that a supervisor had a duty to adequately supervise a supervisee's activity and failed to complete that duty. If a client or the supervisee was damaged in some way by the supervisor's failure to adequately perform, then the supervisor was negligent. There may also, depending on individual state statutes, other mandated activities and responsibilities that the supervisor is obligated to perform. Failure to perform these activities may carry specific legal penalties and fines.

If a supervisor fails to perform appropriate supervisory activity, she can have direct liability in the event that a supervisee or client is damaged. This could include failing to adequately monitor or supervise a supervisee's activity, giving an inappropriate treatment directive, allowing a supervisee to operate outside her scope of practice, failure to listen carefully to a supervisee, or a biased or unfair evaluation.

Even if a supervisor performs competently, they may be found liable if damages occur to a client at the hands of one of their supervisees through the principle of vicarious liability. Numerous court cases have established the obligation and liability of supervisors to perform appropriately.

CHAPTER SIX
Risk Management
Strategies

Serving as a supervisor elevates your legal risks. As the supervisor, you are responsible for the work product of supervisees who legally become the "hands and legs" (agent) of the supervisor. Supervisors should take supervision seriously, because of the risks that it creates. As with many situations in life that involve potential liability, there are a number of things the individual supervisor can do to minimize legal risks. Falvey, (2002) developed a list of the **Top 10 Risk Management Strategies for Supervision:**

1. Maintain Written Policies
2. Monitor Supervisees Competence through Work Samples
3. Supervision Contract
4. Be Accessible, Dependable, and Available
5. Informed Consent for Supervision
6. DOCUMENT, DOCUMENT, DOCUMENT
7. Consult with Others Appropriately
8. Know the Law and Administrative Regulations
9. Discuss Ethical Codes
10. Liability Insurance

Recepuro & Rainey (2007) developed a practical list of ten things that supervisors can and should do to minimize potential liability.

1. Consider developing supervision guidelines or a supervision contract.

2. When assigned a new supervisee, make inquiries to determine if there are any special concerns about a particular supervisee.

3. Follow up on complaints or concerns about a supervisee promptly and thoroughly. Documenting steps taken to resolve the problem may further reduce risk.

4. Develop an informed consent form for supervisees to sign, indicating they understand what is expected of them.

5. Establish and maintain appropriate supervision boundaries.

6. When the supervisee is providing therapy associated with increased risk, more intensive supervision may be appropriate.

7. Review charts of clients in treatment with supervisees. Develop a regular schedule for chart review.

8. Establish regular hours for supervision and adhere to them.

9. Establish routine guidelines for supervisees related to the management of suicidal or violent clients.

10. Document all supervision sessions. Take notes, and encourage supervisees to take notes as well. Ask supervisees to develop reports or to keep a supervision journal.

Supervisors can reduce their legal risks by prudent "hiring," planning, and monitoring. A simple risk management strategy would be to require a formal application process with appropriate documentation. Conduct other research before accepting an individual as a supervisee, including investigating employment gaps or discontinuity in training. It's also advisable to conduct a thorough background check, including a criminal record search. Asking for references from prior supervisors or employers to determine a potential supervisee's ability to get along with others and to adapt to rules can prevent a supervisor from agreeing to supervise a "loose cannon" or "walking lawsuit."

Prudent supervisors do as much as possible to structure and organize supervision. This can prevent problem situations from developing. Spending the time to clarify a supervisee's expectations about supervision as well as informing them of the supervisor's expectations is also an outstanding preventative measure.

Many issues can be clarified in advance and problems prevented through developing a formal supervision contract and an informed consent agreement for supervision. Taking supervision seriously, meeting regularly, correcting ongoing problems, responding to request for help, keeping supervisory notes, and obtaining regular supervision of supervision can significantly limit the risk of problems and potential liability.

Supervisors can reduce their legal risks by having a working knowledge of their supervisee's caseloads and by doing a careful assessment and screening of clients. The supervisor should conduct an initial assessment of the supervisee's competence and assign cases to a supervisee consistent with their ability and skill level. Another way of managing risks is to ensure that the supervisor consistently monitors the supervisee's caseload to determine significant changes in the cases. What often might start off as a "vanilla" case has the potential to turn into a particularly complex situation that may be beyond a supervisee's competence.

Giving clients direct access to the supervisor through the provision of a phone number or e-mail address can be another way to ensure that the supervisor is knowledgeable about what is going on in a particular case situation. Another strategy for minimizing potential liability is for the supervisor to accept only cases within their area of competence for their supervisees. Attempting to supervise a case that you do not have competence to provide services yourself opens you up to potential liability.

The 800 Pound Gorilla in the Room

Many supervisors have the experience of being cognizant that things may not be going well in supervision and make a conscientious effort to address the issues that could be causing problems in supervision. Other supervisors may be very aware of the fact that there are problems in service provision or problems in the supervisory relationship, but choose to ignore the issues and "let sleeping dogs lie."

Supervisees may be reluctant to bring up problems in the supervisory relationship due to the power differential and the potential risk of "being seen as a problem." In both situations, the supervisor and supervisee "ignore the 800 pound gorilla in the room" and continue the process of supervision without fully addressing issues that are impacting the supervision and/or service provision.

There are a number of issues in supervision that may be difficult to address openly and completely due to the inherent nature of the relationship, role conflict, or administrative control. Anxiety on the part of the supervisee about how they are performing can cause a distortion in the dynamics and the level of honesty and objectivity within the relationship. Cultural, age, and gender issues necessarily compound the relationship if not discussed openly and honestly. Personal issues, lifestyle choices, habits, or lack of a sense of professional identity may complicate supervision and have a direct impact on service provision.

Transference and countertransference issues complicate an already complicated relationship in very unusual and subtlety distorted ways. Organizational issues and climate may require certain behaviors on the part of the supervisor or supervisee that go beyond the norm of professionalism. These can become very formidable issues to deal with in supervision. It may also be particularly troublesome for a supervisor to address issues of burnout, lack of responsiveness to clients, and the impact of personal issues on professional services as they may be more of a matter of the supervisor's judgment rather than concrete standards.

Another, more subtle, issue that can be difficult to address in supervision is dress and appearance. This is particularly true for supervisees who make choices about personal appearance that are outside the norm of the work culture. These issues need to be addressed not as a matter of personal preference on the supervisor's part, but as to how they may impact clients and service delivery.

For many supervisees, documentation is their "Achilles' heel." While arguments can be made that a supervisee who fails to document services is still providing quality services, documentation is a part of professional behavior. Tying documentation back to the impact that a lack of documentation might have on a client or the organization may be the most effective way to address this issue. Other difficult issues to address in supervision might include the relationship between the supervisor and supervisee, differences in theoretical perspectives, cultural differences, and differences in personality or lifestyle.

There are a number of strategies that can be employed to make dealing with problematic issues and complicated supervision issues more effective. Generally speaking supervisors should attempt to depersonalize the issue and always connect the issue back to client care. Making the issue less of a personal opinion or value judgment, and more about how it is impacting services, will hopefully allow supervisees to respond to issues based on their professionalism, and not based on the power differential. Make the issue or problem a situational one and not a character flaw when addressing issues with supervisees.

Involving the supervisee in addressing the issues can minimize resistance. Asking for the supervisee's perception of the problem or the issue and brainstorming potential solutions with the supervisee are effective ways of dealing with the issue. Processing anger, anxiety, or resistance in the context of the impact that the issue has on services may allow the supervisee to get the most out of the supervision. It may be necessary for the supervisor to reiterate the purpose and goals of supervision and develop an action plan with specific steps that will result in a resolution of the problem. Compartmentalizing the problem to one aspect of performance rather than focusing on broad issues is generally more palatable to the supervisee and will result in more effective change.

Summary

Risk management strategies can assist supervisors in minimizing their elevated liability risks. Developing supervisory contracts, informed consent agreements, and assessing a supervisee to determine the level of competence and expertise, reviewing records on a regular basis, establishing protocols for managing high risk clients, and documenting supervisory sessions are particularly effective in managing risks inherent in supervision.

Having written policies and procedures for supervision, consistently monitoring changes in a supervisee's caseload, carrying appropriate liability insurance, and maintaining appropriate supervisory boundaries can also minimize liability situations from occurring.

Issues may occur with supervisees that may be difficult or unpleasant to deal with. Ignoring these problems is not a good "risk-management strategy." The personal nature of some issues that occur with supervisees may make open discussion difficult. Cultural, age, gender, lifestyle, burnout, and transference and countertransference issues can create potential liability if ignored or not adequately addressed. No matter how difficult or uncomfortable the issue may be, failure to address the issue puts the supervisor at some risk for liability.

CHAPTER SEVEN

Impairment

In some situations, despite the best efforts of the supervisor, problems may continue to persist beyond reasonable efforts to achieve change or resolution. Some supervisees may not be capable or competent to provide services. Some supervisees may have had issues develop in their life that are impacting their work and their ability to provide services. Some supervisees, for a variety of reasons, may have failed to continue to develop competency as a service provider consistent with current skills and knowledge. In these situations, the supervisor may be faced with making decisions about whether or not a supervisee is impaired to the point that they are harming clients and need to discontinue practicing.

A serious supervisory responsibility is that of "gate keeping," and ensuring that individuals who are no longer competent are not harming clients by continuing to practice. Almost all professional ethics codes address the issue of provider impairment.

"Should a supervisor develop a significant concern about the abilities, philosophical beliefs, or practices of a trainee, the concerns must be shared with the trainee and documented in writing as early as possible." (AAMFT, 2001).

"The supervisor has the authority to enforce and can use sanctions such as a personnel evaluation, reporting to the regulatory body, refusing to recommend for credentials, and others.... The supervisor may need to take actions necessary within his or her scope of authority to lead a social worker out of the profession." (NASW, 1994) ...."should take action through appropriate channels established by employers, agencies, NASW, licensing and regulatory bodies, and other professional organizations." (NASW, 2008) 2.09 b.

"Supervisors are encouraged to serve as gatekeepers by monitoring for personal or professional limitations.....likely to impede future professional performance." (ACES, 1993).

"Supervisors should be aware of any personal or professional limitations of supervisees, which are likely to impede future professional performance. Supervisors have the responsibility of recommending remedial assistance to the supervisee and of screening from the training program, counseling setting, or state licensure those supervisees who are unable to provide competent professional services." (ACA, 2005) C.2.g,

"Regardless of qualifications, supervisors do not endorse supervisees who may be believed to be impaired in any way that would interfere with the performance of the duties associated with the endorsement." (ACA, 2005) F.5.d.

Serving as a gatekeeper to ensure the quality of professional services can be a very difficult, but essential component of clinical supervision. "Gate keeping" and dealing with the impaired supervisee is a critical, albeit challenging, aspect of a supervisor's responsibility" (Johnson et al.,

2008). The supervisor's task as a gatekeeper is to distinguish between what is a problem in learning versus an impairment. Personal problems, skill deficits, mental health issues, or characterological issues can present obstacles to professional functioning (Ladany, Friedlander, & Nelson, 2005). Averholser and Fine (1990) identified four types of professional incompetence: 1) lack of knowledge, 2) inadequate clinical skills or technical skills, 3) poor judgment, and 4) disturbing interpersonal attributes.

Lamb et al. (1991) defined impairment as "an interference in professional functioning" that is reflected in one or more of the following ways:

➤ An inability or unwillingness to acquire and integrate professional standards into one's repertoire of professional behavior;
➤ An inability to acquire professional skills to reach an acceptable level of competence;
➤ An inability to control personal stress, psychological dysfunction and/or excessive emotional reactions that may affect professional functioning."

In an earlier article, Lamb et al. (1986) further differentiated between competent and impaired supervisees. One indication of an impaired supervisee is an individual who does not acknowledge, understand, and/or address the problem after it is identified. Another indication of impairment may be a problem with a supervisee that is not merely a reflection of a skill deficit or is not restricted to one area of professional functioning. A supervisor might begin to think in terms of impairment when a supervisee typically requires a disproportionate amount of time on the supervisor's part. Impairment might be indicated when the supervisee's behavior does not change as a consequence of feedback, remediation, or allowing additional time for personal and professional development.

Once a supervisee has been identified as potentially impaired, it is incumbent on the supervisor to address the specific issues that are felt to result in an impaired level of performance. A number of strategies are open to the supervisor at that point. It would be important to identify, in writing, and as specifically possible, how the individual supervisee's impairment is impacting client services. At that time, the supervisee should be given the opportunity to obtain remediation for specific skill deficits. A plan of action for remediation should be committed to writing, ensuring that the supervisee's due process rights are honored. It may be appropriate in some circumstances, particularly if interpersonal or personal issues are resulting in an impaired level of performance, to allow for a leave of absence. The process of identifying an impaired supervisee, developing a plan for remediation, or requiring a leave of absence is a legally high risk activity on the part of the supervisor. It may be prudent and appropriate to consult with other supervisors, personnel specialists, or experienced colleagues to ensure that the supervisor is on firm legal, professional, and ethical footing.

Summary

Some situations go well beyond the nature of a problematic supervisee. Supervisors may be faced with situations in which a supervisee is actually impaired and beyond reasonable efforts to change or rehabilitate. In these situations, the supervisor must serve as a "gatekeeper" to protect clients and the profession. Determining if a supervisee is impaired, is a difficult task that a supervisor must undertake with considerable thought and perspective. Particular attention must be given to due process rights and documentation of attempts at remediation.

CHAPTER EIGHT
Evaluation

Supervisors are ethically bound to provide an impartial, objective, and accurate evaluation of supervisees. Supervisees are legally entitled to receive an unbiased and objective evaluation of their skills and performance. The supervisor's lack of understanding of the significance of their role as an evaluator can often lead to formal complaints on the part of supervisees. The lack of timely feedback has become the most common basis for a formal ethics complaint regarding supervision (Koocher and Keith-Speigel, 1998).

A supervisor's reluctance to deal with uncomfortable evaluation issues has potential legal implications, as it may relate to a supervisee's ability to obtain employment or licensure. Supervisors must understand that evaluation is an ongoing process and not an event, i.e., a once a year performance appraisal. Continuous evaluation by supervisors provides supervisees an opportunity for remediating particular skill deficits or improving specific aspects of performance. How the evaluation/feedback is handled is the core to a positive or negative supervisory experience (Lehrman and Ladany, 2001).

Evaluation is a four step process that begins long before the supervisor sits down with a rating form to prepare a formal appraisal. The initial step in the evaluation process should take place the first meeting of a supervisor and supervisee. Establishing goals and objectives for supervision, as well as spelling out specific criteria on which the supervisee will be evaluated, should occur at the beginning of the supervisory process, and preferably in writing.

Supervisors should receive ongoing feedback as to how they are performing on these criteria as a regular part of the supervisory sessions. Providing more formal feedback at set intervals, such as once a quarter or the end of each semester, insures and documents that the supervisee has been made aware of the level of their performance. This may be particularly essential in those situations where the final evaluation, which formalizes performance for a specific time period, is going to be negative or critical. Providing more formal evaluation, at definite time intervals, puts the supervisee on notice and eliminates any "surprises" in the evaluation.

It may be worth the supervisor's time to examine and reflect on their own experiences of being evaluated. What factors or circumstances might have kept the evaluation from being a constructive experience? Identifying the format and the process of evaluation at the time of orientation provides understandable expectations and transparent criteria for acceptable service provision. The format, methods, and techniques that will be a part of the evaluation process should be known in advance by all parties.

In some situations, it may be advisable to clarify who will be involved in the evaluation, particularly if information is to be solicited from another staff member or other supervisors. Attempting to be as clear and as concrete as possible and describing in behavioral terms exactly what the supervisee will be evaluated on can go a long way towards eliminating difficulties in evaluation. The focus of the evaluation needs to be on behaviors, not on personality factors or on the personal preferences of the supervisor.

Falendar (2004) makes a distinction between Formative Feedback and Summative Assessment. Formative Feedback has, as its purpose, the focus of attempting to assist in skill development. This is done primarily by the identification of issues that impede clinical practice with clients or issues that impede the growth and development of the supervisee. Formative Feedback is offered by the supervisor as a means to take corrective action that would improve the quality of service delivery and promote skill development.

Freeman (1985) identifies a number of characteristics of Formative Feedback including the fact that it is ongoing and occurs throughout the period of supervision. It is typically informal and not documented in personnel files or as a part of a formal evaluation. Formative Feedback should be consistent, objective, reliable, and timely, provided in close proximity to the actual event. The information in Formative Feedback should be clear, descriptive, constructive, and developmentally appropriate for the supervisee's experience level.

Conversely, Summative Evaluation is an objective measure of the competence level of a supervisee and typically covers a pre-designated time period (Falendar, 2004). Normally, Summative Evaluation is a quantifiable rating on specific goals and objective of performance. Summative Feedback or Evaluation increases liability issues, as these documents are often the basis for employment, promotion, tenure, or credentialing. Since Summative Evaluation can have employment and career implications, formal evaluations incur ethical and legal liability for supervisors. This is particularly true if it can be established that the evaluation was handled improperly and directly caused damages to the supervisee.

Summative Evaluations can be particularly difficult if they result in an overall negative appraisal. It is incumbent on the supervisor to be sure that they have defined the criteria for success clearly and in advance and that they have documented frequent formative feedback and assistance in problem areas. Utilizing multiple methods of evaluation and having data other than simply self-report and case consultation can minimize the potential problems of an adverse evaluation.

If a Summative Evaluation is going to be negative, it is always advisable to consult with another supervisor or obtain supervision of your supervision. Finally, be prepared for a negative reaction by the supervisee, particularly in terminations. It is important to gauge your reactions and limit your comments. Always ask yourself the question. How would the particular comment that I am about to make sound in court or before a licensing board?

Summary

A key component of supervision is the evaluative component that must inevitably occur.
Supervisees are entitled to a fair, unbiased and objective evaluation based on clearly established criteria. Failure to provide an accurate evaluation opens the supervisor to potential liability. Formative evaluation is an integral part of the ongoing supervisory process. The summative evaluation covers a specific period of time and is a quantifiable rating on specific goals and objective of performance. Summative evaluation increases liability issues, as these documents are often the basis for employment, promotion, tenure, or credentialing.

Bibliography

American Association for Marriage and Family Therapy. (2001). *AAMFT code of ethics*. Alexandria, VA.

American Association of Pastoral Counselors (2009). Supervision Standards. In *Membership standards and certification manual* (pp. 32-33). Fairfax, VA.

American Counseling Association (2005). *American Counseling Association Code of Ethics*. Washington, DC.

American Psychological Association Trust (2006). *Assessing and managing risk in psychological practice*. Rockville, MD: The Trust.

American Psychological Association Ethics Committee (2008). Report of the Ethics Committee, 2007. *American Psychologist, 63,* 452-459.

Association for Counselor Education and Supervision (1995). *Ethical guidelines for counseling supervisors.*

Association of State and Provincial Psychology Boards. (2003). *Supervision guidelines*. Montgomery, AL: Author.

Behnke, S.H., Preis, J., & Bates, R.T. (1998). *The essentials of California mental health law. New York: Norton.*

Bennet, B.E., Bryant, B.K., Vandenbos, G.R., & Greenwood, A. (1990). *Professional liability and risk management.* Washington, DC: American Psychological Association.

Bernard, J.M. (1997). The discrimination model. In C.E. Watkins (Ed.), *Handbook of psychotherapy supervision.* New York: Wiley.

Bernard, J.M., & Goodyear, R.K. (2004). *Fundamentals of clinical supervision (*3rd Ed.). Boston, MA: Pearson.

Bernard, J.M., & Goodyear, R.K. (2009). *Fundamentals of clinical supervision (*4th Ed.). Boston, MA: Pearson.

Bordin, E.S. (1983). A working alliance based model of supervision. *The Counseling Psychologist,* 11, 35-42.

California Board of Psychology. (2008). *Laws and regulations booklet.* Sacramento, CA.

Campbell, J. (2000). *Becoming an effective supervisor: A workbook for counselors and psychotherapists.* Philadelphia: Accelerated Development.

Campbell, J. (2006). *Essentials of clinical supervision.* New York: John Wiley & Sons, Inc.

Canadian Psychological Association. (2000). *Canadian code of ethics for psychologists. (3rd Ed.)*

Celenza, A. (2007). *Sexual boundary violations: Therapeutic, supervisory, and academic context.* Lanham, MD: Jason Aronson

Disney, M.J., & Stephens, A.M. (1994). *The ACA Legal Series (Vol. 10): Legal issues in clinical supervision.* Alexandria, VA: American Counseling Association.

Fallendar, C.A., & Shafranske, E.P. (2004). *Clinical Supervision: A competency based approach.* Washington, D.C.: American Psychological Association.

Falvey, J.E. (2001) *Managing clinical supervision: Ethical practice and legal risk management.* Pacific Grove, CA: Brooks-Cole.

Frawley-O'Dea, M.G., & Sarnat, J.E. (2001). *The supervisory relationship: A contemporary psychodynamic approach.* New York, NY: Guilford Press.

Freeman, E. (1985). The importance of feedback in clinical supervision: Implications for practice. *The Clinical Supervisor.* 3, 5-26.

Glaser, R.D. & Thorpe, J.S. (1986). Unethical intimacy: A survey of sexual contact and advances between psychology educators and female graduate students. *American Psychologist, 41, 43-51.*

Griffith, B.A., & Freiden, G. (2000). Facilitating reflective thinking in counselor education. *Counselor Education and Supervision.*

Gottlieb, M.C., Robinson, K., & Younggren, J.N. (2007). Multiple relations in supervision: Guidance for administrators, supervisors, and students. *Professional Psychology: Research and Practice,* 38, 241-247.

Guest, P.D., & Dooley, K. (1999). Supervisor malpractice: Liability to the supervisors in clinical supervision. *Counselor Education and Supervision, 38, 269-279.*

Guthell, T.G., & Gabbard, G.O. (1993). Obstacles to the dynamic understanding of therapist patient sexual relationships. *Amer5ican Journal of Psychiatry,* 150, 188-196

Hammel, G.A., Olkin, E., & Taube, D.O. (1996). Student-educator sex in clinical and counseling psychology doctoral training. *Professional Psychology: Research and Practice, 27, 93-97.*

Handlesman,, M.M., Gottlieb, M.C., & Knapp, S.C. (2005). Training ethical psychologists: An acculturation model. *Professional Psychology: Research and Practice, 36,* 93-97.

Harrar, W.R., VandeCreek, L., & Knapp, S. (1990). Ethical and legal aspects of clinical supervision. *Professional Psychology: Research and Practice.*

Harris, E. (2003, September). *Legal and ethical risks and risk management in professional practice: Sequence I.* Symposium conducted by the Minnesota Psychological Association, St. Paul, MN.

Haynes, R., Corey, G., & Moulton, P. (2003). *Clinical supervision in the helping professions: A practical guide.* Pacific Grove, CA: Brooks/Cole.

Hensley, L.G., Smith, S.L., & Thompson, R.W. (2003). Assessing competencies of counselors-in-training: Complexities in evaluating personal and professional development. *Counselor Education and Supervision.* 42(3), 219-230.

Inman, A.G. & Ladany, N. (2008). Research the state of the field. In A.K. Hess, K.D. Hess, and T.H. Hess (Eds., *Psychotherapy supervision: Theory, research, and practice (2nd Ed., pp. 500-520)* Hoboken, NJ: Wiley.

Johnson, M.T. (1995). Case examples of supervisor liability. *Monitor, 26,* 15.

Johnson, W.B., Forrest, L., Rodolfa, E., Elman, N.S., Robiner, W.N.,& Schaffer, J. (2008). Addressing professional competence problems in trainees: Some ethical considerations. *Professional Psychology: Research and Practice, 39,* 589-599.

Kaiser, T. (1997). *Supervisory relationships: Exploring the human element.* Pacific Grove, CA: Brooks/Cole.

Kitchner, K.S. (1988). Dual role relationships: What makes them so problematic? *Journal of Counseling and Development, 67, 217 – 221.*

Knapp, S. J., & VandeCreek, L. (2006). *Practical ethics for psychologists: A positive approach.* Washington, DC: American Psychological Association.

Koocher, G.P., & Keith-Speigel, P. (1998). *Ethics in psychology: Professional standards and cases.* New York: Oxford University Press .

Lamb, D.H., & Catanzaro, S.J. (1998). Sexual and non-sexual boundary violations involving psychologists, clients, supervisees , and students: Implications for professional practice. *Professional Psychology Research and Practice.*

Ladany, N., Lehrman-Waterman, D., Molinaro, M., & Wolgast, B. (1999). Psychotherapy supervisor ethical practices: Adherence to guidelines. *The Counseling Psychologist, 27, 443-475.*

Ladany, N., Friedlander, M.L., & Nelson, M.L. (2005). *Critical events in psychotherapy supervision: An interpersonal approach.* Washington, DC: American Psychological Association.

Lazarus, A.A., & Zur, O. (2002). *Dual relationships in psychotherapy.* New York: Springer.

Lehrman-Watterman, D., & Ladany, N. (2001). Development and validation of the evaluation process within supervision inventory. *Journal of Counseling Psychology.* 48(2), 168-177.

Lowe, S.M. (2010). Sharing wisdom: Ethnic-minority supervisor perspective. *Training and Education in Professional Psychology, 4,* 3-69.

Martino, C. (2001). *Secrets of successful supervision: Graduate students' preferences and experiences with effective and ineffective supervisors.* Symposium at American Psychological Association, San Francisco, CA.

Munson, C.E. (1993). *Clinical social work supervision.* New York: Hayworth.

NASW (1994) *Guidelines for Clinical Social Work Supervision.*

NASW (2008). Code of Ethics

Navin, S., Beamish, P., & Johnason, G. (1995). Ethical practices of field based mental health counselors. *Journal of Mental Health Counseling, 17, 243-253.*

Nelson, M.L., & Freidlander, M.L. (2001). A close look at conflictual supervisory relationships: The trainee's perspective. *Journal of Counseling Psychology*, 48 (4), 384-395.

Pope, K.S., & Vasquez, M.J.T. (1998). *Ethics in psychotherapy and counseling.* San Francisco: Jossey-Bass.

Reaves, R.P. (1998). *Avoiding liability in mental health practice.* Association of State and Provincial Psychology Boards

Recupero, P.R. and Rainey, S.E. (2007). Liability and risk management in outpatient psychotherapy supervision. *Journal of the American Academy of Psychiatry Law, 35 (2, 188-195.)*

Remley, T.P., & Herlihy, B. (2005). *Ethical, legal, and professional issues in counseling.* Upper Saddle River, NJ Merrill/Prentice Hall.

Saccuzzo, D. (1997). Law and psychology, *California Law Review, 34 (115), 1-37.*

Saccuzzo, D. (2002). *The Psychologist's Legal Update # 13:Liability for failure to supervise adequately: Let the master beware (Part 1).* National Register of Health Service Providers in Psychology.

Simmons v. United States, 805 F 2d 1363 (9th Cir. 1986)

Stoltenberg, C.D., & McNeil, B.W. (1998). *IDM supervision: An integrated developmental model for supervising counselors and therapists.* San Francisco: Jossey-Bass.

Stoltenberg, C.D., & McNeil, B.W. (2009). *IDM supervision: An integrated developmental model for supervising counselors and therapists (3rd Ed.).* New York, NY: Routledge.

Storm, C.L., & Todd, T.C. *The reasonably complete systemic supervisor resource guide.* Boston: Allyn and Bacon.

Stromberg, C. & Dellinger, A. (1993). Malpractice and other professional liability. *The Psychologist Legal Update.*

Tuckman, B.W., & Jensen, M.A. (1977). Stages of small group development revisited. *Group and Organizational Studies, 2*, 419-427.

Thomas, J.T. (2010) . *The ethics of supervision and consultation.* Washington, DC: American Psychological Association.

Yorke, V. (2005). Bion's "vertex" as a supervisory object. In C. Driver & E. Martin (Eds.), *Supervision and the analytic attitude (pp. 34-49).* London, England: Whurr Publishers.

Watkins, C.E., Jr. (1997). *Handbook of psychotherapy supervision.* New York: Wiley.

Zakrewski, R.F. (2006). A national survey of the American Psychological Association student affiliate's involvement and ethical training in psychology-educator student sexual relationships. *Professional Psychology: Research and Practice, 37,* 724-730.

Clinical Supervision: Legal, Ethical and Risk Management Issues

Post Test

1. Campbell (2006) has stated that supervision includes all but the following key element:
    a) Monitoring a practitioner's work to increase their skills
    b) Solving problems in order to provide clients the optimal service quality
    c) Complying with statutes and mandates
    d) Prevent harm from occurring to clients

2. All the following are myths commonly held about clinical supervision, except:
    a) If I am an experienced counselor or therapist, I will be an effective supervisor.
    b) Supervision is only for beginners or the inexperienced
    c) Supervision is a skill that cannot be trained or developed
    d) Because supervisors are professionals, diversity issues do not have to be addressed

3. Consultation occurs when a case is discussed between
   a) Two pairs of equal status
   b) A senior and junior staff peers
   c) A supervisor and a supervisee
   d) a and b

4. Haynes et al (2003) identified the components of a competent supervisor as:
   a) Trained in supervision
   b) Are trained in the areas of services being supervised
   c) Comfortable being in an evaluative role
   d) A and B
   e) A, B, and C

5. Martino (2001) reported that the most frequently reported quality of the "worst supervisor" was:
   a) A supervisor who acts unethically
   b) A supervisor who is inflexible
   c) A supervisor who lacks interest in supervision
   d) A supervisor who was punitive or overly critical

6. Martino (2001) reported that the most frequently reported quality of the "best" supervisor was:
   a) Clinical knowledge and expertise
   b) Providing useful feedback
   c) Empathic
   d) Ethical

7. Munson (1993) wrote an article where he outlined what he called the "Supervisee's Bill of Rights." It contained all but the following:
   a) A growth oriented supervisor
   b) Extensive experience
   c) Supervision at regular intervals
   d) An evaluation based on criteria made know well in advance

8. Clinical supervisors are more focused on all but the following:
   a) Developing their supervisee's skills
   b) Increasing the supervisee's competency
   c) Providing cost effective and efficient services
   d) Increasing a supervisee's knowledge about functioning ethically
   e) Increasing a supervisee's professional development

9. The Holistic Model of supervision
   a) Focuses on the supervisor being the "expert"
   b) Builds on the existing strengths of the supervisee
   c) Eliminates psychopathology in supervisees
   d) None of the above

10. Bernard and Goodyear (2009) state that administrative supervision likely focuses on:
   a) Personnel policies
   b) Ethical Service Provision
   c) Fiscal Policies
   d) A and B
   e) B and C
   f) A and C

11. Disadvantages of group supervision encompass:
   a) Having to manage the dynamics of the group
   b) Increasing the number of perspectives and ideas
   c) Confidentiality Issues
   d) A and B
   e) B and C
   f) A and C

12. Evaluation is a four step process that begins long before the supervisor sits down with a rating form to prepare a formal appraisal and includes:
   a) Establishing Goals and Objectives
   b) Specifying the criteria that will be used for evaluation in advance
   c) Providing ongoing feedback on a consistent basis
   d) All the above

13. Activities identified by Campbell (2006) required for Ethical Supervision include all the following except:
   a) Having been trained in supervision
   b) Carrying liability insurance
   c) Obtaining Informed Consent for Supervision
   d) Regular supervision of your supervision
   e) Knowledge of current Ethics Code

14. Definition of competency to supervise varies from discipline to discipline, but most have common components, including:
   a) Formal education,
   b) Professional training
   c) Carefully supervised experience.
   d) All the above

15. Pope and Vasquez (1998) indicated that the most frequent reason for ethical complaints being filed with the state board of psychology was:
   a) Sexual or dual relationships
   b) Unprofessional, unethical, negligent practice
   c) Convictions of crimes
   d) Improper or inadequate supervision

16. The following organization specifically prohibits supervising family members

    a) American Association of Marriage and Family Therapists
    b) National Association of Social Workers
    c) American Psychiatric Association
    d) American Psychological Association
    e) All the above

17. Pope and Vazquez (1998) identified different forms of competence in supervision, including:
    a) Intellectual competence
    b) Emotional competence
    c) Spiritual competence
    d) a and b
    e) a and c

18. A *boundary crossing* is a term that describes:
    a) A departure from commonly accepted clinical practice that is unethical
    b) A departure from commonly accepted clinical practice that is ethical
    c) A departure from commonly accepted clinical practice that is neither necessarily ethical or unethical
    d) A violation of professional ethics

19. Ethics codes that have specific prohibitions regarding sexual contact with supervisees and students include all but the following:
   a) American Psychological Association
   b) American Psychiatric Association
   c) American Association of Marriage and Family Therapists
   d) National Association of Social Workers

20. The following is not one of **The Seven Deadly Boundary Crossings in Supervision** Guthell & Gabbard (1993)"
   a) Money
   b) Gifts
   c) Bartering
   d) Physical contact

21. Lazarus and Zur (2002) would make an argument that a sexual relationship between two consenting adults, who happen to be supervisor and supervisee
   a) Is not necessarily problematic
   b) Can never be truly consensual
   c) Is always unethical
   d) b and c

22. A recent study by Zakrewski (2006) reported rates of sexual contact between supervisors and supervisees at
   a) 20%
   b) 10%
   c) 2%
   d) Less than 1%,

23. Some social interactions between supervisors and supervisees may be incompatible with a supervisor's duties because:

   a) They may cause supervisors to lose sight of their evaluation responsibilities
   b) The danger of a perception of favoritism
   c) Possible loss of objectivity toward a supervisee
   d) All the above

24. Supervision of a particular supervisee may be complicated by a supervisee's:

   a) Personal issues
   b) Lifestyle choices or habits
   c) Lack of a sense of professional identity
   d) All the above

25. Averholser and Fine (1990) stated that all but the following are aspects of professional incompetence, *except*:

   a) Lack of knowledge,
   b) Inadequate clinical skills or technical skills,
   c) Poor judgment,
   d) Poor financial management
   e) Disturbing interpersonal attributes.

26. The **standard of care** is;

   a) A rather loosely defined and constantly changing,
   b) A gradually emerging principle regarding the practice of a profession
   c) A principle of law dating back to the Constitution
   d) Both a and b

175

27. Fallendar and Shafranske (2004) identified Standards of Care for Supervision as including all but the following:
a) Supervising only within your area of competence
b) Reviewing and co-signing cases
c) Consistent monitoring and controlling supervised activities
d) Accurately documenting supervisory activities
e) Consistent and timely supervision.

28. There is case law that would indicate that supervisors can be liable:
a) For what they knew about the actions of a supervisee
b) Situations where they should have known a supervisee was acting inappropriately
c) Only for their direct actions
d) Both a and b

29. Vicarious liability holds that supervisors are liable for their supervisee's actions because
a) They are in a position of responsibility and authority,
b) The supervisee was under the direct control of the supervisor,
c) The supervisor, or supervisor's agency or organization, may profit from the actions of their supervisees
d) All the above

30. Falvey, (2002) developed a list of the **Top 10 Risk Management Strategies for Supervision** which included all but the following:
   a) Monitor supervisees competence through work samples
   b) Supervision contracts
   c) Accept only 8 supervisees at a time
   d) Document supervision

31. Difficult issues to address in supervision might include:
   a) The relationship between the supervisor and supervisee,
   b) Differences in theoretical perspectives,
   c) Cultural differences
   d) All the above

32. Supervision of a particular supervisee may be complicated by a supervisee's:
   a) Personal issues
   b) Lifestyle choices or habits
   c) Lack of a sense of professional identity
   d) All the above

33. Ladany, Friedlander, & Nelson, 2005 state that obstacles to professional functioning might include:
   a) Personal circumstances
   b) Academic deficits
   c) Mental health issues
   d) All the above

34. Supervisors can reduce their legal risks by:
- a) Having a working knowledge of their supervisee's caseloads,
- b) Cconducting an initial assessment of the supervisee's competence
- c) Monitoring the supervisee's caseload to determine changes in flux of the cases
- d) All the above

35. Formative feedback has the following characteristics:
- a) Ongoing throughout supervision
- b) Informal
- c) Timely
- d) Constructive
- e) All the above

I, _____
(name of participant) affirm that I am the person who completed this home study and am responsible for this post test.

Signature:

_____

_____

Continuing Education Credit is available for reading these materials and passing the Post Test at a level of 70 percent.

Send the completed and attested Post Test along with a check for $50.00 to:

Foundations: Education and Consultation
1400 B Browns Lane
Louisville, KY 40207

A certificate for four hours of Continuing Education Credit will be issued within seven days of receipt.

73247972R00109

Made in the USA
Lexington, KY
07 December 2017